WHITE SETTLERS IN TROPICAL AFRICA

Lewis H. Gann and Peter Duignan

GREENWOOD PRESS, PUBLISHERS
WESTPORT, CONNECTICUT

Library of Congress Cataloging in Publication Data

Gann, Lewis H   1924-
    White settlers in tropical Africa.

    Reprint of the 1962 ed. published by Penguin Books,
Baltimore, which was issued as WA13 of Penguin African
series.
    Bibliography: p.
    1. Africa, Eastern--Race question. 2. Africa, West
--Race question. 3. Nationalism--Africa, Eastern.
4. Nationalism--Africa, West. I. Duignan, Peter, joint
author. II. Title.
[DT365.42.G36 1977]   325'.24   76-49445
ISBN 0-8371-9394-X

A Greenwood Archival Edition—reprint editions of classic works
in their respective fields, printed in extremely limited quantities,
and manufactured to the most stringent specifications.

Originally published in 1962 by Penguin Books, Baltimore

Reprinted with the permission of Lewis H. Gann & Peter Duignan

Reprinted in 1977 by Greenwood Press, Inc.

Library of Congress Catalog Card Number 76-49445

ISBN 0-8371-9394-X

Printed in the United States of America

CONTENTS

PREFACE

THE nineteenth and twentieth centuries will be recorded by future historians as the age of great white migrations. From all parts of Europe a stream of settlers poured into North and South America, into Australia and New Zealand, into what is now Israel, and into the vast eastern land mass comprising present-day Soviet Asia. Some Frenchmen, Spaniards, and Italians settled on the northern shores of the African continent, but Tunisia, Algeria, Tripolitania, Cyrenaica, and Morocco, though geographically a part of Africa, historically belong to the Mediterranean basin; furthermore, they are separated from Black Africa by a great belt of deserts.

White emigrants also went to South Africa, where they now form a racial minority surrounded by a non-European majority. So many Europeans have settled in the Union of South Africa, and so deep has their impress on that country been, that the Union can no longer be looked upon as part of Black Africa proper.

This book is concerned with the history and problems of those Europeans who pushed farther inland and settled between the Limpopo River, the Union of South Africa's north-ernmost boundary, and the highlands of Kenya, the northern limit of white settlement in tropical Africa. The majority of the white settlers in Black Africa have made their homes in the Federation of Rhodesia and Nyasaland. Accordingly, more space has been devoted to those territories than to any of the others. The Union of South Africa has only been dealt with in so far as its problems impinge directly on the countries farther to the north. In writing this very general introduction to the problems of white settlement in Africa, the authors have tried to keep aloof from current local politics, only touching on these issues in so far as they seemed essential for an understanding of the questions under discussion.

The writers would like to acknowledge advice and criticism

Preface

from Mr T. W. Baxter, Director of the National Archives of Rhodesia and Nyasaland, Mr. E. E. Burke, Principal Archives Officer, Dr M. Gelfand, C.B.E., Federal Medical Services, Mr M. Faber, University College of Rhodesia and Nyasaland, Dr Carl Brand and Dr Bruce Johnston of Stanford University, California, Mr P. A. C. Laundy, Librarian of the Legislative Assembly of Southern Rhodesia, and Mr J. H. M. Beattie, Oxford University. They are also indebted to the *Central African Examiner*, the *New Leader*, and the *National Review* for permitting them to make use of material previously published in those journals. The opinions and judgements expressed here represent only those of the authors.

CONTRASTS IN BLACK AND WHITE

AFRICA is on the march. Great social and economic revolutions are shaking the continent from Cape Town to Bizerta; and as Africa is changing, so are our ideas regarding its inhabitants. In Victorian times the Africans' stock stood low. In the words of a worthy Baptist missionary, 'lying, stealing, gluttony, polygamy, licentious debauchery, and cannibalism' were all second nature to the natives, who represented a lower stage of human evolution, and who were undoubtedly getting worse from generation to generation. Without the whites' Gospel, the blacks were thought to be lost. The indigenous Africans, Europe's 'external proletariat', were looked upon as being even more licentious and improvident than her 'internal proletariat', the unskilled workers of Manchester, Lille, and Essen; for most Victorians, this was saying a great deal.

These wholehearted condemnations of the Bantu-speaking peoples are not difficult to understand.* Most descriptions of old Africa came from missionaries, who regarded the precepts of Victorian middle-class morality as absolute. They usually identified themselves with the views of contemporary businessmen who provided most of their funds. The missionaries believed that men should work so as to save money and improve themselves; the Africans did neither and, consequently, appeared to their critics as 'a nation of unemployed'. African tribal systems, devoid of economic individualism and in the grip of 'kingly socialism', seemed morally wrong.

The missionaries also stood for the Western ideal of monogamous marriage and premarital chastity. The Africans had

---

* It should be noted that many nonconformist preachers in the nineteenth century condemned many of the customs of Catholic Portuguese, or even of Welsh peasants, in the same unmeasured terms as they denounced those of Africans.

different ideas on the subject, and to most missionaries African family-systems, based upon polygamy, seemed vicious. The early Western observers of Africa also thought in terms of European chivalry. Many of them came from Victorian households where housewives had maids and were not expected to do the heaviest work. Critics of Africa were therefore liable to conclude that the native woman, who hoed her husband's field, was nothing but the chattel of her lustful and idle man, a view not quite in accordance with the facts.

The old-time missionary's grim picture of Africa was strengthened by the impressions of other Europeans in Africa. The Victorian period was the great era of explorers in Africa, who produced bulky, well-illustrated travelogues of little-known countries. From these massive tomes, the tribal African usually emerged in an equally unfavourable light.

The early explorers' task in Africa was desperately difficult. Isolated in the wilderness, shaken by fevers, the traveller usually had to depend on African carriers for the transport of his supplies. These hired men did not necessarily share their master's love of adventure. They might go on strike or desert, and when they did, the result was sometimes catastrophic. In any case, the pioneers of geography had to make their way through strange countries and had to deal with strange peoples whose languages they rarely understood.

The indigenous tribes' reception of the white strangers was sometimes hostile and, what was worse, always unpredictable. The traveller, unfamiliar with the complicated network of tribal family-relationships or 'international' politics, which he unwittingly became involved in, often could see neither rhyme nor reason in the Africans' doings. Sometimes the natives were friendly and sold food; sometimes they were hostile and showered poisoned arrows on their visitors; obviously they were not guided by reason; they were 'savages' and could not be trusted.

As Africa was gradually colonized, the missionaries' and explorers' impressions were reinforced by those of other Europeans. Late-nineteenth-century soldiers and colonial administrators joined in criticizing primitive Africa. These Victorian servants of Empire were, after all, faced with the tremendously difficult task of policing huge areas with tiny military forces. They had to run territories as large as the whole of England on budgets fit only for English parishes. They had to cope with slave traders, warlords, and tough adventurers in search of easy money. They saw that peace was essential to Africa's future progress, and they knew that at the time there was no real alternative to their authority. To them, primitive society was an ever-present reality, not the subject of an academic investigation undertaken sixty or seventy years after the effective pacification of Africa. No wonder that the early Empire-builders tended to be harsh in their judgements.

If the administrators were inclined to criticize indigenous methods of government or their absence, the European settlers complained of African economic methods. The farmer who half a century ago began to grow tobacco in some lonely spot on the Rhodesian veld had little use for the old-style native villager. The white pioneer could not improve his farm or build better roads as long as his native neighbours continued to practise their age-old shifting cultivation of the slash-and-burn variety; the colonist could not breed superior cattle as long as the tribesman's small and diseased beasts were allowed to graze next to his sleek dairy herds. Above all, the white man needed black labour, and the supply of the commodity seemed mostly inadequate, especially when the harvest had to be gathered and a whole year's gruelling work might be ruined because no 'boys' would turn up.

The white miner's predicament was a similar one. The gold mine and the coal pit needed an ever-growing number of unskilled workers. There was not enough white labour to go round. Even where the whites were willing to dig the shafts themselves, their services were found to be too expensive, which meant that black men had to be employed. In the early days, however, before the taste for European cloth, pots, and pans had become universal, the native villagers were often unwilling to work for wages; or, what was nearly as bad from the employer's point of view, the tribesmen would only work in their own agricultural 'off-season' which naturally coincided with the white farmer's. The problem of industrial incentives, which is still with us even in the most highly developed economies, often seemed insoluble to the pioneer-miner or the early engineer, who thus joined the throng of critics condemning African society.

Generalizations are always dangerous, and especially where race attitudes are concerned. There were Victorian observers, such as David Livingstone, who were as detached in their diagnosis of native society as in their appraisal of some physiological phenomenon. There were also Victorian missionaries who took a more considerate view of native society than the damnation-and-hellfire preacher and who knew how to distinguish between different social structures. The graduate of a nineteenth-century ecclesiastical training-college might be unfamiliar with theoretical anthropology, but he knew his Old Testament inside out, and the Third Book of Moses provided him with an incomparably good account of the ways of cattle-keeping nomads. White farmers and hunters who settled in the interior became little chiefs or patriarchs, and sometimes liked and respected African ways. But, in the balance, the views of such people were less effective than those of the critics whose views fitted in well with the self-congratulatory optimism of contemporary Europe.

The cultural barriers were too great for any real understanding, and the Europeans from overseas were always handicapped because there seemed to be no social group in an African classless society with whom they could truly identify themselves. A Scottish merchant in Beirut might despise 'natives' in general, but he was quite willing to make a special case for an old Syrian merchant family with whom his firm had traded for generations. An English army officer would look down on a Bengali clerk but not on a Rajah. In Africa, the situation was much more difficult, though even here there was a tendency for British officials to make some exceptions, say for Barotse aristocrats who worked a complex state machinery and were described as running an equivalent of the British constitution, complete with Sovereign, Lords, and Commons, in Darkest Africa.

Those who were ready to condemn the African tended to exalt the white settlers. There are scores of late-Victorian and Edwardian novels which tell of clean-limbed, sunburnt, young Englishmen who set out to make their fortunes in Africa and build a new country. These colonists stood for more than just making money; they represented Queen and Empire, civilization and Christendom. Something of these attitudes survives amongst Europeans settled in East and Central Africa. The romanticized version of the white colonist also continues a shadowy existence in Hollywood, where great white hunters, lean and muscular, make their way through steamy jungles, accompanied nowadays by a beautiful blonde as well as a faithful black gun bearer.

The climate of opinion is changing; the African's stock is going up, while that of the European colonist is going down. There are many reasons for this dramatic reversal. First of all, there is a general reaction against imperialism itself. Critics of colonial expansion were never lacking, even in the heyday of late-Victorian imperialism; colonies were expensive; they only benefited a small number of privileged investors in the know; they led to foreign complications and war. These theorists gained a wider public after the South African War.

Far more shattering still was the impact of the First World War, which produced a violent hostility to the beliefs sacred to most Victorians, the businessman's standard of values, the glorification of economic individualism, the ideals of family life. The attack against middle-class standards came from many different quarters. Socialists criticized the economic basis of private enterprise, arguing that capitalism led to imperialism, and imperialism led to war. New schools of psychology came into being whose votaries subjected Victorian moral codes to a scathing analysis, whilst many of their lesser followers came to deny that basic assumption, so brilliantly put into words by Winston Churchill, that 'the stern compression of

13

circumstances, the twinges of adversity, the spurs of slights and taunts in early years are needed to evoke that ruthless fixity of purpose and tenacious mother-wit without which great actions are seldom accomplished.'* Some psychologists, in their criticism of Western man burdened by inhibitions and frustrations, even began to idealize primitive societies whose members were supposedly living 'in a world which we have long since forgotten, a world in which the whole of nature was filled with the divine breath of life.'† The craze for Harlem and for jazz, for the gay, happy, and uninhibited Negro of the slums (who never existed outside the white dreamer's imagination), also became a marked feature of the twenties; it formed part of a wider trend, a sophisticated escapism which led many intellectuals to denounce Western mechanical civilization and to flee into a world of their own making, where simplicity and irrationality, sometimes even violence and nihilism, were exalted at the expense of the harder 'bourgeois' virtues.

The reaction against nineteenth-century values also affected Western attitudes towards the subject-races of the Victorian world. Many Victorians identified the Africans in some ways with 'the lower orders' in their own society; so did their descendants, but now the Africans gained from the comparison, for everything that was not bourgeois became praiseworthy.

The Second World War and its aftermath – the division of the world into two hostile blocs, anxiously watched by a group of neutralist nations – further contributed to a mood of disillusionment that caught hold of many intellectuals. The Western colonial empires disintegrated like the Austro-Hungarian monarchy after 1918, their place being taken by numerous successor states, each of which now quickly tried to furnish itself with the customary equipment of national independence, including a national airline, and a new anti-colonial mythology to account for the country's past ills.

* Winston S. Churchill, *Marlborough, His Life and Times*, London (Cassell), 1933-8.
† C. G. Jung, *Essays on Contemporary Events*, London (Kegan Paul), 1947, p. 65.

The new mythologies in turn influenced intellectuals overseas.

There were also changes in economic thinking about Africa. Earlier theorists used to view the white settlers as producers of essential raw materials and gave them praise. The world slump, however, had brought about a glut of raw materials, and Rhodesian farmers were no longer regarded as the benefactors of England. The end of the slump restored the settlers' position as producers, but by now the potentialities of African peasant-farming had come to be looked upon with greater understanding. Peasant-farming in fact was one of those economic expedients that often appealed to the Right and Left alike in England, and its possibilities were sometimes exaggerated. By contrast, the European farmer's role in Africa appeared less valuable. In addition, European industrial exporters rediscovered the possibilities of African mass markets; they looked upon black men with new respect as potential customers, while white settlers, who were less numerous, now appeared of less consequence when it came to marketing British merchandise.

The outlook on Africa was further changed by the development of the social studies. This trend became particularly noticeable after the Second World War, when social studies became as popular as psychology had been after the First. The new outlook was especially influenced by the rise of modern anthropology.

The study of primitive society was originally the preserve of the chair-borne student. A writer, sitting in some European library, laboriously pieced together accounts from sea captains, missionaries, and travellers who told of the strange customs of outlandish tribes. These reports were analysed, and the various social systems grouped according to some preconceived scheme of social evolution. Bushmen came at the bottom – Bradford businessmen came out at the top. But gradually the scissors-and-paste scholars gave way to those who were prepared to study primitive man at first hand; under the impact of Malinowski and Radcliffe-Brown for example, in the nineteen-twenties, anthropologists spent long periods amongst the tribes whom they wished to study, and indeed became almost naturalized citizens of 'their' people. The new approach resulted in major contributions to scholarship and greatly extended our knowledge of primitive races and of social problems in general.

At the same time, this new work helped to put primitive folk into a more favourable light, even though anthropologists usually pretended to 'objectivity' and freedom from value-judgements. In practice, the anthropologists' observations often resulted in a new set of value-judgements, sometimes shrouded by a complicated terminology. Under the new dispensation, the 'noble savage', that dream-figure of eighteenth-century philosophers, sometimes reappeared in the guise of 'preliterate man' who was supposed to have lived in a state of balanced social equilibrium before the whites came and upset the apple-cart.

The general swing in opinion with regard to primitive people in Africa was also linked to some extent with a major change in the social composition of white opinion-makers on the African continent itself. Sixty years ago, most intellectual work in Africa was done by missionaries; and it was their accounts which probably most influenced public opinion in Europe.

The early missionary, like the early settler, had to be a man of all trades. He busied himself with preaching and teaching, with linguistics and anthropology; he was his own builder, carpenter, and often enough a hunter or a farmer as well. He took it for granted that he was to be a leader of the new African churches for a long time to come. After the First World War, however, the missions often found it more difficult to secure staff and funds from a disillusioned and impoverished Europe. Even when there was no actual decline, help from overseas did not keep pace with the dramatic expansion of African church membership. The missionaries, accordingly, were forced to rely increasingly on African personnel and African money, in addition to government subsidies. The white missionary tended to become a supervisor and a specialist, convinced of the need of ecclesiastical devolution of power, and often friendly towards African aspirations in the political field.

The place of the missionary writer was taken more and more by the graduate specialist concerned only with a limited range of problems, a man whose ideal was one of intellectual integrity rather than of service to God, and whose ambition lay in the direction of a professorial chair rather than of an episcopal see. Specialization, as in so many other fields, led to greater efficiency and outstanding achievements.

But the new opinion-makers, the intellectuals, also became more divorced from the ways of thinking of the other Europeans whom they met in Africa. The old-time missionary never doubted that white farmers and businessmen were excellent people whose work should be encouraged – provided, of course, that they were Christians. Modern intellectuals frequently reacted in a different way. While the African was looked upon with a new respect, the white colonists were despised, in many cases, as being intellectually or academically inferior. Some intellectuals began to imagine, quite mistakenly, that running a tobacco farm or a chain of kaffir stores was somehow a less difficult or responsible occupation than writing a dissertation or a novel. A good many academics, in fact, took over that very attitude towards 'trade' which they professed to despise in the minor gentry of old.

When Doris Lessing, the well-known novelist and playwright, tells of the depths to which a Rhodesian can sink, she writes of a Jewish friend of hers, a Communist. Having been in Rhodesia for some time, he stopped thinking about the World Revolution and no longer studied the Marxist classics, all highly respectable, non-economically-motivated occupations. Instead the Jew decided to beat the thick-skinned Philistines at their own game, became a prosperous business man, married a rich girl – and proceeded to mimic the oily voice of a big-time huckster.* By going into trade, the Jew had not really performed an economic service to his adopted country – he had simply given up his ideals and become corrupted – an assumption that Jane Austen's characters would have shared

* Doris Lessing, *Going Home*, London (Michael Joseph), 1957.

17

with Doris Lessing. Such an attitude is fundamentally based on the view that in a country like Rhodesia no European can really help making money, a belief that is oddly parallel with the old-time missionary's mistaken conviction that bountiful nature and the labours of his wives would assure every black man an easy but sinful living on the veld.

It is easy to overdo the argument. There were many intellectuals who did not accept this rather naïve view of social relationships in the colonies. Not all whites in Africa, moreover, were condemned; the technician on short-term contract, a labour migrant like many of the academic men in Africa, escaped much of the current censure. The earlier frontiersman, a person not particularly admired by his Victorian contemporaries, similarly came into his own. The old trekker, unlike his supposedly degenerate modern offspring in the towns, is now often depicted as a virtuous, simple primitive – like the Bantu – an interpretation that takes little account of the trekker's true economic function in the past. * The man who really 'takes the rap' as far as Central Africa is concerned, however, is the white immigrant of today, the man who mines copper in Luanshya, repairs motor-cars in Nairobi, grows fruit trees near Umtali, or opens a hosiery business in Bulawayo. Certain writers, like Mannoni, have even enlisted Freud and tried to attribute the white man's reactions in a colonial situation to a peculiar mental make-up, a theory that takes no account of the economic realities of emigration.

Various elements have now crystallized into a new postcolonial orthodoxy that dominates much of contemporary thinking on Africa and offers a new crusading issue to radicals disillusioned with the old fighting causes at home.† Some

* See S. Patterson, *The Last Trek: A Study of the Boer People and the Afrikaner Nation,* London (Routledge and Kegan Paul), 1957, where this point of view is argued with much sociological knowledge, and little realism.

† The myth of British moral leadership is an attempt to replace the prestige of Empire by a new kind of prestige. But Britain has rarely possessed moral leadership, and her claims to it have always been loathed by foreigners, even more than her material claims.

white settlers would go even further and argue that Africa has become a vast screen upon which some intellectuals project their own guilt-feelings, demanding reforms and sacrifices from others in the name of a superior morality, without having themselves to pay the price for these changes. However this may be, a good deal of the censure which European colonists now receive in Africa is certainly as highly charged emotionally as the old-style missionary's condemnation of tribal Africans, and as much divorced from sociological reality. The whites are like the blacks in that they have both been shaped by historical and economic conditions. High-powered sermons are not enough. Men should also be understood in terms of their environment and social heritage. The roots of their being lie in history, and for a better understanding of the settlers' problems one must turn to Africa's past.

Chapter 1

THE HISTORICAL BACKGROUND

EXPLORERS AND SLAVE TRADERS

The first European pioneers in tropical Africa came from the Iberian Peninsula. Between 1442 and 1485, daring Portuguese navigators reached Sierra Leone, secured a base on the Gold Coast and penetrated to the Congo estuary. In 1488 the Portuguese effected an even more memorable achievement. Bartolomeu Diaz rounded the Cape of Good Hope. His expedition formed part of a grand design to secure the reputedly fabulous trade of the Indies, to outflank the Muslims firmly established in the Eastern Mediterranean, and to gather more souls to the Catholic faith.

There were even more speculative projects. Extraordinary tales were told that the land of Ophir from where King Solomon had got his gold was somewhere in Africa as was the lost kingdom of Prester John, a great Christian ruler. Prester John would help the Portuguese in their struggle against the Mohammedans and in their search for wealth.

More and more Portuguese adventurers followed in the footsteps of Diaz, and in the sixteenth century they opened the route to India, established themselves at various points along the East African coast, defeated their Arab competitors in the Indian Ocean by their superior naval technology and fighting skill, and gained a virtual monopoly of the African export trade in gold, ivory, gum, and other goods. In addition, the Portuguese secured footholds on the West coast (for a short time) but, like their English and Dutch competitors of later years, they soon found serious difficulties in establishing their commerce in Africa.

Penetration inland was impeded by the absence of good ports and by the vagaries of a tropical climate. The Portuguese only managed to settle at a few points along the low-lying coastal plains and in the Eastern Zambezi Valley, areas riddled by tropical diseases that no doctor then knew how to cure. The malarial mosquito proved a worse enemy than the Muslim's scimitar or the African's spear; and Portuguese manpower was insufficient to colonize their vast maritime empire effectively.

The indigenous peoples of East Africa, moreover, had few wants, and unlike those of West Africa they did not subsequently succeed in producing any crops suitable for export on a large scale. Even had the Bantu done so, East Africa lacked great waterways, navigable from the ocean far into the interior, whereby merchandise could be cheaply transported.

For many centuries, accordingly, Africa remained a 'continent of outposts'.* Native civilizations, such as the remarkable Zimbabwe culture in Southern Rhodesia, rose and perished, but effective contact with Europeans remained limited. The African interior continued to be regarded as a land of fabled lakes and mythical mountains of gold. Africa did have one source of real wealth – the manpower of its own people. At first the trade in slaves was very limited. A few thousand captives were taken from West Africa to Portugal before the end of the fifteenth century, but many more were sold on the slave marts of the Near East as domestic retainers and concubines. The rise of great plantation economies in the New World gave an enormous impetus to the trade; Englishmen, Frenchmen, Dutchmen, Danes, Swedes, and Brandenburgers, all joined in the new commerce. Slave trading was not only profitable in itself, but also gave rise to numerous other industries to supply the needs of African sellers, and became part of a network of trade linking Europe, Africa, and the New World. The exported slaves mostly became agricultural labourers. They grew the sugar, coffee, tobacco, and cotton required by the Old World in ever-increasing quantities. In exchange, Africans acquired muskets, knives, cloth, beads, and other luxury goods.

* The phrase is taken from S. H. Frankel, *Capital Investment in Africa*, London (Oxford University Press), 1938, p. 30.

More important still was the addition to the African diet which resulted from contact with the strangers from overseas. Maize, peanuts, manioc (cassava), sweet potatoes, and citrus fruit are all said to have been brought to Africa by the Portuguese, while the Arabs were probably responsible for the introduction of bananas, rice, onions, and some varieties of grains.

But Africa had to pay heavily for its contacts with foreign traders. It was only at the beginning of the nineteenth century that the slave trade began to decline. The traffic in human beings had been increasingly opposed by evangelical and humanitarian reformers. Then, too, the commerce was highly speculative in nature, and entrepreneurs were just as likely to go bankrupt as to make their fortunes. Industrialization, moreover, wrought profound changes in the structure of the European trade. The slave-traders on the West coast were replaced by a new kind of dealer, often quite as tough as his predecessors, but interested in agricultural products rather than slaves. By the end of the eighteenth century, Western European living standards were slowly rising, and there was an increased demand for better illumination at night, as well as a greater vogue for personal cleanliness. West Africa was able to produce the palm oil and palm kernels needed by the European candle and soap industries. The wider use of machines in English and foreign factories required more lubricants, which West Africa began to supply. Machines turned out more goods; these goods required new markets, and some merchants began to look towards Africa to expand sales. The whole commercial edifice on which the European slave trade had rested, therefore, began to disintegrate.

This process was furthered by disinterested political action, inspired by idealistic more than economic motives. In 1804 the Danes made an honourable start by abolishing the slave trade; an example followed by Britain and the United States in 1808, and subsequently by all the great seafaring nations, though the British Navy played by far the largest share in hunting down the remaining slave ships. Partly as a result of being cut off from their labour supplies, partly for internal economic and political reasons, the great plantation-economies of the New World, founded on one-crop culture and slavery, gradually went to pieces. In 1833 slavery came to an end in the British West Indies; the United States got rid of it as the result of the great civil war between the slave-owning South and the industrial North; in Brazil, slavery was forbidden in 1888. The 'Christian' slave trade disappeared, and the great African migration to the other side of the Atlantic came to an end.

The whites were not, however, the only ones to engage in this shameful traffic. European enterprise in the main had centred on the West coast of Africa, but most of the East coast trade was in Arab and African hands. In the nineteenth century slaves were increasingly exported to the clove plantations of Zanzibar, Pemba, and Réunion. Blacks were also shipped to the markets of Southern Arabia and Persia. Slaves (as the cheapest means of transportation available to non-industrialized societies) were employed as carriers under conditions where the dreaded tsetse fly and topographical obstacles made the employment of animal-drawn vehicles either too costly or altogether impracticable.

The trade in ivory was often linked to the commerce in slaves. Ivory was used for the manufacture of a large number of goods, such as piano keys, billiard balls, ornaments, and fans. The steady expansion of the European luxury industries in the nineteenth century gave a considerable impetus to the trade. Africa became the world's most important supplier of elephants' tusks. As the great beasts became scarcer along the coast, the Arabs pushed further inland. Sometime around 1840 they were firmly established on Lake Tanganyika, and about the middle of the last century they had gained a commercial foothold in Uganda. By the 1860s they were trading on the upper reaches of the Congo and along Lake Nyasa. Meanwhile Muslim adventurers were pushing into the interior from the north, up the Nile Valley, and trading with some of the Nilotic and Nilo-Hamitic races whom they encountered.

The Portuguese rivalled the Arabs as slavers. The growth of the slave trade in Portuguese East Africa appears to have been linked to the decline of local industries, such as the production of gold-dust and the cultivation of sugar. The traffic in human beings became so profitable that local labour supplies were disorganized. Professional cut-throats in the nineteenth century raided inland through the valleys of the Zambezi and the Luangwa. Many slaves were sent to Mauritius. When the transoceanic slave trade was stopped, mainly as the result of British pressure, there still remained opportunities for the raiders to get rid of their wares on the great estates, known as *prazos*, that stretched along the Zambezi and throughout other parts of Portuguese East Africa.

In Angola the Portuguese, many of whom were mulattoes, dealt in ivory, later in wild rubber, and, of course, in slaves. Slaves were sold first to Brazil, then to the cocoa plantations of São Tomé. Like their Arab competitors, the Portuguese-speaking traders paid for their purchases in cloth, beads, muskets, and gunpowder. Unlike the Muslims, who began in the end of the last century to set up independent little principalities in the interior, the West coast traders never aimed at independent political power. Instead, they preferred to support indigenous chiefs, who raided their neighbours for slaves to sell to the strangers.

The African tribes reacted in different ways to this new and terrible challenge. The Umbundu of Angola became enterprising traders on their own account; as did the Yao of Nyasaland, who combined their mercantile activities with conquest of land for the sake of permanent settlement. Others, like the Bemba of Northern Rhodesia, became agents of the slave traders and attacked their weaker neighbours for the purpose of selling prisoners in exchange for guns. In the course of these campaigns, it often happened that the victims of the raids also acquired firearms and in turn hit on the idea of selling *their* captives. The trade extended further and further like a contagious disease, especially where Africans themselves practised domestic slavery. The weaker tribes appear to have been incapable of an active response to this raiding system.

On the other hand some African peoples did not participate

in the international slave trade to any large extent. These included the comparatively civilized Barotse, who lived in the fertile Upper Zambezi Valley of North-western Rhodesia. The Barotse kingdom was based on a relatively developed economy, which depended on agriculture, fishing, and cattle herding. Each of the Barotse subject tribes participated in a complex network of intertribal exchange with some specialized product of its own. The Barotse Valley was not densely populated, and the ruling aristocracy, therefore, attempted to import rather than to export manpower, either by encouraging voluntary immigration, or by raiding, or by levying human tribute. The warlike Matabele, settled (about 1837) in what is now Southern Rhodesia, similarly abstained from slave trading. Originally of Zulu origins, the Matabele constituted the most powerful and warlike tribe south of the Zambezi, but instead of selling their prisoners to foreign dealers they dragged them back to Matabeleland. The Matabele depended on war to replenish their herds with cattle and to strengthen their manpower by the constant incorporation of prisoners into the tribal structure.

American writers have shown how the importation of guns and horses to the great plains of North America made warfare a much more ferocious affair than it had been in the olden days, when warriors had to rely on home-made weapons. New Zealand historians have also come to similar conclusions with regard to the introduction of firearms among the Maori; and the 'new warfare' amongst the Bantu of Africa had similar consequences.

The fact that some tribes would not sell their prisoners to strangers was a matter of small comfort to their weaker neighbours. For no matter where the raiders came from, or what their precise object was, the effects of their campaigns appear to have been devastating. With the extension of raiding from the coasts, the 'gunpowder frontier' swept into the interior of Africa, introducing great changes into the indigenous tribal structures. There seems little doubt that the slave and ivory trade, the consequent importation of muskets and rifles, as well as the development of new systems of military tactics among some of the African peoples, made warfare more destructive. It is impossible to give exact figures, but all contemporary observers had similar tales to tell. Richard Burton, a well-known explorer, estimated for instance that one caravan, merely to capture fifty-five women, destroyed at least ten villages, each with a population of between a hundred and two hundred souls. Many were killed in battle; more died on the long grim march to the coast. The survivors who managed to escape from the raiders would be in equally desperate plight; the destruction of their villages and crops might be accompanied by famine and disease. Even if none of these things happened, there was bound to be a general disorganization of tribal life as the result of the permanent loss of so many able-bodied workers.

The slave trade, Africa's primary form of labour-migration, was a grimly expensive affair. The effects of war cannot merely be measured in absolute terms. They must also be seen in relationship to the recuperative powers of the society in which these armed clashes took place. The power of recovery possessed by a Bantu tribal community, with its meagre social surplus, was small – much smaller than that of the modern, highly industrialized economies of Western and Central Europe, which have withstood the effects of two terrible wars with astonishing resilience. The new warfare in Africa, by contrast, proved too much for the simple subsistence economies that had to carry the weight of this fighting. With or without foreign conquest the old accustomed ways were doomed, and new forms of political and social organization became indispensable to Africa.

THE SOUTH AFRICAN FRONTIER

The Arab and Portuguese adventurers who converged on the interior of Africa during the nineteenth century were reinforced by another group of immigrants who came from the south. The story of the southern invaders started in 1652, the year in which the Dutch East India Company sent out Jan van Riebeeck to establish a settlement on Table Bay, on the extreme southern tip of Africa. The Dutch did not aim at colonization. They merely intended to secure a port of call where their ships might obtain fresh water and much-needed provisions on the long route to the East Indies. A fort was built to protect the market-garden and cattle-trading site, but expansion was discouraged. Soon it became evident that a farming community was essential to the development of the growing colony. Old servants of the Company received grants of land, so that they might produce grain, meat, and wine to supply the Cape garrison and the crews of the many sailing ships that dropped anchor at the Cape. Later, in 1679, a number of families moved beyond the isthmus of the Cape proper, and this process of expansion continued. The original settlers, mostly from Holland and Northern Germany, were joined after 1685 by French Huguenots, who had been forced to leave their homes as the result of religious persecution.

As the colonists pushed deeper and deeper inland, they began to take to pastoral rather than arable farming. The pressure of population increased, and the numerous sons of Boer families found it difficult to make a living in Cape Town, where most of the skilled work was done by Malay slaves. Subdivision of land, accompanied by more intensive cultivation, was not a feasible proposition, as long as capital was scarce. The best way for a poor man to get on in life was to make his way to the frontier. Here the Boers took to cattle-keeping of an extensive type. This mode of production was best suited to the conditions which they encountered in the interior, where capital and labour were scarce, markets were few, and only the supply of land seemed unlimited. The Boers kept trekking in order to avoid competing with their neighbours for pastures and wells; trekking also got rid of boundary quarrels. The frontiersmen's extensive methods of cultivation, moreover, exhausted the soil, 'the veld got tired'. So, like the African farmer, they had to move on.

White Settlers in Tropical Africa

The frontiersmen were never self-sufficient, and even on the extreme edge of settlement they depended on articles such as guns, wagons, tea, coffee, and cloth, which had to be bought from outside. The best means of paying for this merchandise was by driving cattle to the market, for the town was now a long way off and cattle possessed the great advantage that they could walk to market. There were a few goods of small bulk and high value, such as soap, candles, beeswax, and ivory, that could be transported to the Cape by expensive, slow-moving ox-wagons. The frontier possessed other attractions for the adventurous *trekboer*; he could hunt wild animals, trade cattle from the indigenous tribes, and secure more native labour. Overland migration was made easier when itinerant traders (*smouses*) supplied the frontier with a moving market – farmers no longer had to waste their time by taking their wares to Cape Town. *

First the *trekboer* supplied the Cape market; later the centre of economic gravity shifted more towards the new ports that were opened on the east coast. Port Elizabeth, East London, and Durban became the most advanced points of departure for inland expansion. By this time the trekkers themselves belonged to a new nation, no longer 'Dutch', but speaking a new language, Afrikaans, a derivative from Dutch. The Afrikaner was a different type of person from the earlier placid Dutch farmer with his skill for intensive farming. The *trekboer* became one of Africa's foremost wilderness-specialists. Rough and illiterate as he often was, the Afrikaner adjusted to frontier conditions that would have completely baffled his ancestors. He knew how to handle a span of oxen in rough country; he became knowledgeable as a 'soil prospector', wise to the ways of finding the best farming land in the wilderness; he turned into a crack shot and an expert huntsman. The interior held no terrors for him, and he was always ready to eke out a

*See S. D. Neumark, *Economic Influences on the South African Frontier, 1652-1836*, Stanford (University Press), 1957. A somewhat different interpretation is P. J. van der Merwe's brilliant study, *Trek: Studies oor die Mobiliteit van die Pioniersbevolking aan die Kaap*, Cape Town (Nasionale Pers Beperk), 1945.

hard living by 'transport-riding' or by other subsidiary occupations, such as making rhino whips for sale.

The trekkers also developed a highly specialized system of military tactics, based, like those of the Czech Hussites of old, on the employment of wagon-*laagers* (defending themselves from within a closed circle of wagons). The Boer's wagon came to serve both as a means of transport and as a means of defence. The use of *laagers* was combined with the employment of mounted sharpshooters who, though lacking discipline, proved excellent fighters on their own ground. The Boers' military skill easily defeated Bushmen and Hottentots. Later, the Afrikaners met far more warlike opponents among the Bantu tribes, who were pushing into Southern Africa. In 1778 the Kaffirs were encountered for the first time at the Great Fish River, and the Governor of the Cape then entered into an agreement with the African chiefs that the river should be the boundary between Dutch and Bantu settlements. The treaty, however, was soon transgressed, and in 1781 the Bantu suffered a serious defeat in the first of a long series of grim clashes between these two competing groups of pastoralists.

The Dutch settlers were subsequently reinforced by a new stream of immigrants from Great Britain. In 1795, during the war with revolutionary France, the British occupied the Cape. When peace was made, the Cape was returned to Holland, but hostilities broke out again, and in 1806 the British reoccupied the Cape permanently. The end of the Napoleonic Wars was followed by a disastrous economic depression, and industrial unemployment led to the first organized scheme of British settlement in South Africa. In 1820 British settlers, including professional men, market gardeners, husbandmen, and labourers, landed in Algoa Bay. The theorists who had planned the scheme thought in terms of a relatively compact settlement, based on small farms cultivated intensively; but the project was not well thought out. A large number of the colonists were not suited for farming, and the small holdings of 100 acres which they each received proved inadequate for their support under South African conditions.

White Settlers in Tropical Africa

Many colonists abandoned their holdings and made their way to the towns, where they provided a considerable stimulus to economic development. Others stuck it out on the land and adjusted themselves to local ways of farming. The 1820 settlers were followed by small numbers of additional colonists from Britain, some of whom went to Natal; some immigrants also came from Germany. The more daring spirits pushed further into the interior as hunters, traders, and pioneer-farmers, and an English frontiersman came into existence, as hardy and experienced as the Afrikaner, whose ways he began to adopt.

In the meantime the Boers were steadily advancing inland. The most dramatic incident in the course of their frontier history was the Great Trek, which began in 1835. The Trek was preceded by many journeys of hunters, traders, and stockmen beyond the Orange River. To the economic attractions of migration, there were now also added political and administrative incentives. The emigrants, still legally British subjects, were discontented with many aspects of British rule. They objected to the emancipation of the Hottentots; they distrusted most British missionaries, and they considered themselves insufficiently protected against the depredations of local cattle raiders. Relations were further embittered by the abolition of slavery at the Cape, and the inadequate way in which many former slave-owners were compensated for the loss of their property. The end of slavery was a particularly serious matter for some of the wealthier farmers, who found great difficulties in working their farms in the accustomed way as long as they were within the sphere of British jurisdiction. They now joined their poorer compatriots in search of an easier living on the frontier.

Slavery was not, however, the main issue. The pastoral Boer economy required, after all, only a very limited number of bondsmen, and differed in this respect greatly from, say, the cotton-economy of the American South, or the clove-economy of Zanzibar. In South Africa, two wholly different sets of beliefs, customs, and political ideals came into conflict, for egalitarian as the Boers were amongst themselves, they would accept neither political nor ideological interference from overseas, nor equality with the non-Europeans at home. They also considered themselves gravely misrepresented abroad. 'We complain', wrote Piet Retief, one of the most prominent of the trekkers, in 1834, using words that were to echo again and again in later years from Cape Town to Nairobi, 'of the unjustified odium that has been cast upon us by interested and dishonest persons under the name of religion, whose testimony is believed in England to the exclusion of all evidence in our favour, and we can foresee as a result of their prejudice nothing but the total ruin of our country!'*

The Great Trek was the Boer frontiersman's Declaration of Independence. Admittedly, its effects should not be exaggerated. A large number of Afrikaners did not trek and preferred to stay where they were under British rule. The Western Cape, with its wealthy wine-farmers, continued to maintain a different tradition, partly because here the warlike Bantu was not a problem, and the unskilled labourers were mainly coloured people of mixed parentage, generally speaking Afrikaans, rather than displaced or dispossessed African tribesmen. Nevertheless, the centre of gravity of the Afrikaner nation to some extent began to swing to the north. By the end of 1837, some 5,000 men, women, and children had crossed the Orange River, the northern boundary of the Cape Colony. The trekkers continued through what later became the Orange Free State, and made their way into the Northern Transvaal. A group of Boers also tried to set up a republic in Natal; but this area was accessible to British sea-power, as the interior was not, and the Boer attempt in 1843 merely precipitated the annexation of Natal as a British colony. Undeterred, the Boers moved farther to the north. In time they were joined by English-speaking and some foreign-born pioneers. Scottish and Dutch Presbyterian parsons went inland to minister to the

* Some missionaries and humanitarians have viewed the Boers as a kind of unholy scourge, sjambok-wielding hypocrites who, in Livingstone's words, spent their time 'shooting the caffirs, levying their cattle, and making their prisoners slaves'. The contribution of these daring frontiersmen in opening up the high veld was missed.

needs of the isolated Calvinist flocks on the veld. Many of these newcomers married Afrikaans girls; their children tended to adopt their mothers' speech and to become assimilated into the Afrikaner nation.

From the Transvaal, hunters, traders, and prospectors began to make their way into what is now Southern Rhodesia. One of the best known of these pioneers was John Lee, an elephant hunter of mixed English and Afrikaans descent, who in the 1860s acquired a farm in the Mangwe Valley and became a diplomatic agent to the Matabele king, Mzilikazi. Another was Adam Renders, a German-American adventurer, who ran away from his family in the Transvaal and was later found living with the local chief's daughter in an African village near Zimbabwe. A third was George Westbeech, an Englishman, who opened up trade with Barotseland in the seventies. Westbeech and his successors began to compete successfully with the Portuguese and African merchants from Angola who already had established a trade route to the Zambezi Valley. The advance guard of the southern invaders thus made contact with the outposts of the army of intruders from the west, and the ring began inexorably to close on Central Africa.

MARTYRS AND MISSIONARIES

European expansion into Africa presented Christianity with one of its greatest opportunities since the fall of the Roman Empire. The Catholics were the first to take up the challenge, the Jesuits constituting the spearhead of ecclesiastical advance in many parts of the continent. The Society's original purpose was to fight the Reformation in Europe, but the powers of organization, the intellectual ability, the discipline, and self-sacrifice displayed by the Fathers in that great inner-European crisis also made the Order a very suitable instrument for the task of making converts outside the Christian world, in Africa. The Jesuits followed the flag, eager to take the opportunities which the secular authorities provided in Portuguese territory.

The Historical Background

One of the first attempts to secure a Christian foothold in the interior of southern East Africa was made by a courageous Portuguese Father, Gonçalo de Silveira, who sought to convert the Monomotapa, a powerful African chief. Contemporary literature described the Monomotapa as an almost legendary monarch, a kind of second Prester John; actually he headed a Bantu state in what is now Mashonaland. Silveira met with bitter hostility from Muslim traders and excited his host's suspicions so that in 1561 he was executed, the first Christian martyr to die in Southern Africa. Other Portuguese clerics carried Christianity to the valleys of the Congo and the Zambezi, but none of these early efforts were crowned with permanent success.

Protestant missionaries entered the fray later. The eyes of British ecclesiastics were fixed at first on North America, where British settlers stood in urgent need of religious ministration, and in 1649 the Long Parliament passed an ordinance for the purpose of setting up 'A Corporation for Promoting and Propagating the Gospel of Jesus Christ in New England'. Later in the century, missionary work received a further impetus from the movement to set up religious societies in England to combat the 'infamous clubs of Atheists, Deists, and Socinians', whose doctrines were then considered dangerous to Church and State alike.

From converting infidels at home, it was but a short step to evangelical work among unbelievers abroad. The eighteenth century brought a great religious revival, part of a great spiritual wave, emotional rather than intellectual in character, that swept over much of Europe, and affected thought as far afield as the peasant-congregations of the Moravian Brethren, and the itinerant traders and petty artisans in the Jewish ghettoes of Poland. In England, the great revival was closely linked to the process of industrialization. Dissenting groups were ready to preach the Gospel not only in the countryside, but also in the new factory towns that were so often neglected by the older churches. The itinerant preachers, in the true Puritan tradition, taught the forgiveness of Christ, but also the virtues

33

of thrift, sobriety, and hard work. Their dramatic sermons, their love of singing, appealed to the disinherited peasants who had drifted into the grimy slums of Manchester and Glasgow.

Poverty, the dissenters announced, was neither a holy nor an inevitable state; it was something to be overcome by human endeavours. The right way to deal with the problems of society was not by taking up the sword, as fighting Baptists and Fifth Monarchy men had done in Cromwell's days, but by means of individual economic advancement, by making use of the new opportunities that workshops, factories, and counting houses were now beginning to offer in Britain. The nonconformists, like many secular groups of the day, also did a great deal in the cause of charity for children, sick people, prisoners, and slaves, indeed all those who could not be expected to look after themselves in the hurly-burly of free economic enterprise.

In 1787 the Methodists set up a regular system of foreign missions. Eight years later the London Missionary Society was founded with the support of Congregationalist merchants in London. Work was started by the L.M.S. in India, China, and other parts of the world made more accessible by the steady expansion of British trade. This and other religious bodies soon turned their attention to Africa. General interest in the Dark Continent received a great stimulus when the African Association, pledged to further the cause of geographical exploration of the continent, was formed in 1788. The Napoleonic Wars then brought the Cape within the sphere of British influence. In 1803 Dr van der Kemp began to work for the L.M.S. at the Cape, which in time proved a convenient base for further expansion, through Bechuanaland, into the far interior.

One of the greatest of the London Society's missionaries was David Livingstone; no pioneer of Africa ever struck public imagination more than this dour and determined Scotsman. At first sight, the reasons for his enormous appeal are perhaps not quite so obvious. Livingstone assuredly was a very great figure in the missionary world, but the nineteenth century produced scores of outstanding missionary statesmen, such as Robert Moffat, François Coillard, and Robert Laws, who also performed astonishing feats, but whose names are much less well remembered. As a missionary pure and simple Livingstone cannot be compared with François Coillard, the great French Protestant pioneer, who first opened Barotseland to the Gospel. Coillard displayed incredible courage and powers of organization in creating, and helping to find the financial resources for a whole network of mission-stations in a pagan and still inaccessible kingdom. Neither would it be true to say that Livingstone was the greatest of nineteenth-century African travellers, although he performed some astonishing feats. Between 1851 and 1873 he explored many parts of what is now Northern Rhodesia and Nyasaland, and crossed and recrossed the continent. But there were greater African travellers in the nineteenth century, men like Burton, Barth, Speke, and Stanley. Livingstone, in fact, showed less interest in geographical theory than in the more practical problems of exploration, and many of his ideas on the former subject were quite unrealistic.

Still, Livingstone's name became a symbol. The history of his life was one of those great success stories that impressed Victorians so much. Born of a working-class family, he started off in life as a piecer in a cotton-factory, worked his way up to become a doctor, a missionary, and finally a world-famous explorer. Livingstone possessed all the Victorian's faith in scientific progress. He became one of the great pioneers of tropical medicine; and in an age in which most African explorers went down like ninepins, because they did not know how to protect themselves against fevers, Livingstone managed to keep most of the members of his expeditions alive by the effective use of quinine. It is to Livingstone that we owe the first reliable descriptions of medical conditions in Central Africa. One might also argue that it was Livingstone's training as a doctor, with its rigid insistence on accurate diagnostic observation, that contributed much to the value of his observations concerning non-medical subjects, such as ethnography.

In Livingstone's days, medicine had abandoned the metaphysical cast of old, preferring empirical observation to *a priori* reasoning. But much contemporary ethnographic work tended to be cast in a mainly ethical form, and the average missionary account of African ways was apt to be a sermon on African depravity rather than a clinical exposition. Livingstone, on the other hand, was more concerned with recording and analysing native customs, though he did not therefore abstain from making value judgements, and it is instructive to compare his comments on African *mores* with those – say – of Coillard, the self-confessed Micah to the Barotse king.

Livingstone, moreover, helped to formulate a practical policy with regard to tropical colonization. Christianity and commerce, he argued, were bound to go together, for the Gospel could not triumph in Africa without a social and economic revolution. The slave trade must be crushed, unless Africa was to bleed to death. In his own way Livingstone was just as keen an advocate of active European intervention in Africa as Cecil John Rhodes was to become after him. The slave trade could not be beaten by gunboats or by sermons alone, but only by the development of 'legitimate' commerce in the African interior. The Christian Powers, Livingstone was convinced, should expand Africa's wealth and supply the continent with new kinds of goods; by this means African living standards would be made to rise, and the expanding industries of Europe would find new markets and raw materials. Steamships, Livingstone hoped at one time, would some day open up the Zambezi Valley, where great cotton plantations would come into existence, making Lancashire independent of North American supplies. The exchange of manufactured goods for tropical commodities would do away with the commerce in human beings, and the employment of steam transport would end the need for slave porters. These vast changes, however, required some outside force to trigger them off and Livingstone, an ardent imperialist, advocated not merely missionary enterprise, but also British settlement in the heart of Africa.

Livingstone's life-work, followed by a heroic death in the

wilds of Northern Rhodesia in 1873, produced a deep impression on his contemporaries. Victorian Protestantism found a martyr of outstanding stature, and many were ready to follow in his footsteps, despite the appalling dangers from malaria and blackwater fever, the most effective obstacles to penetration inland. New missionary societies were formed to convert, where Livingstone had explored. These included the Universities Mission to Central Africa, a High Church group, founded in response to one of Livingstone's appeals. Its first efforts at settlement on the Zambezi in 1861 resulted in disaster, but later a new attempt secured a permanent foothold in Nyasaland. In 1874 the Scottish Churches commenced work in Nyasaland. Scottish businessmen backed their enterprise by founding the African Lakes Company to supply the missions, to develop trade, and to assist in other ways the tough, independent, small missionary theocracies that had sprung up by the lake side. To the north the London Missionary Society established itself on Lake Tanganyika. The Church Missionary Society, an Anglican body, made new efforts, and in 1877 two of its emissaries were received by Mutesa, the powerful King of Buganda. In the meantime, Livingstone's old Society had also sent pioneers from the south into Southern Rhodesia (then called Zambesia) where in 1859 a mission station was founded at Inyati in Matabeleland.

Protestant missionary fervour also affected the European continent. Partly under Scottish inspiration, the religious revival spread to Switzerland, and from there to France, where the movement benefited from the post-revolutionary revulsion against atheism, as well as the demand for a socially constructive creed. In 1828 the Paris Evangelical Society was founded. Denied access to the French colonies by the Catholic Bourbon government, the Society began to work in Basutoland. Subsequently the Paris Evangelical Society turned its attention to Barotseland, which possessed close linguistic links with the Basuto. Missionary enthusiasm also waxed strong in Scandinavia, and in Germany, especially after the German intrusion into Africa in 1884.

White Settlers in Tropical Africa

The South African back-veld too was stirred. Originally, the Afrikaner farmers had little sympathy with the idea of converting Africans. In the eighteenth century Afrikaners lacked that urban middle class which was giving so much support to missionary work in other parts of the world. Missionary enthusiasm first of all developed amongst the *predikants* of the Dutch Reformed Churches, the nation's intellectuals, and then spread to the laity, subsequently receiving a great inspiration from the remarkable cultural and national development experienced by the Boers after the South African War.

The Catholics took up their old traditions of evangelical work amongst the heathen. In 1868 Archbishop (later Cardinal) Lavigerie, an advocate of French colonization, founded the Order of the White Fathers. The Order took an important share in opening up French North Africa, and then turned its attention to other regions, including Northern Rhodesia and the Congo. The French Fathers were reinforced by recruits from the Netherlands, Germany, and Canada. Jesuits from Northern Europe started in the African missionary field on a large scale in the 1870s. Other Orders joined in the work, and soon Catholic enterprise rivalled that of Protestants in many parts of Africa.

By the end of the nineteenth century the missionary army was well advanced in Africa. A great number of different societies were converging on the African interior, which was generally open to the free enterprise of all. No individual missionary body succeeded in gaining a monopoly, such as that once possessed by the Jesuits in Paraguay. On stations in the lonely African bush Christianity was being preached, churches, schools, and hospitals were being set up, religious training institutions and even workshops and agricultural training farms were started. The missions became little islands of European civilization that contributed towards the promotion of social change among the surrounding tribes. The Gospel and the new learning proved as powerful solvents of indigenous institutions as guns and gunpowder had been. The missions laid the foundations for practically all the religious, educational, and social services that Europe was destined to bring to Africa, and missionaries often played an important part in helping to bring about the new political order that came with the European conquest of Africa.

THE SCRAMBLE FOR AFRICA

Missionaries, traders, and hunters formed the advance guard of white influence in tropical Africa. It was, however, in the last quarter of the nineteenth century that the great European Powers abandoned their previous policy of non-interference and began to stake out effective claims to the interior of the continent. The industrialization of Europe and overseas expansion were closely linked. The growing factories of Birmingham, Essen, and Lille required new markets, more raw materials, and, subsequently, new opportunities for reinvesting past profits.

The spread of industrialization altered the internal balance of power in Europe. Great Britain was no longer the workshop of the world. In the regions around the coal-fields of Western Germany, Belgium, and Northern France (the 'carbon-core' of Western Europe), sprang up great industrial combines. The united German states crushed France on the battlefields of Metz and Sedan, and by 1871 the German Empire was founded; it became the most powerful military and industrial state of Europe and emulated the other Western European Powers by searching for riches overseas. France was thrown on the defensive. No longer the leading continental power, France could not hope unaided to recover from Germany the lost provinces of Alsace and Lorraine. Consolation was found in Africa. The Italians were in a similar position. The numerous Italian states had been moulded into a single kingdom by 1870, and Italy aspired to the status of a great power. Lacking the military or economic resources required for such a role in Europe itself, Italy looked to Africa for the possibility of expansion and greatness on the principle of limited liability.

Africa, 'Europe's last frontier', became not only a battle ground between competing European interests, but also a diplomatic safety valve.

Great Britain throughout most of the nineteenth century was interested in trade, not in political power, and consistently supported foreign régimes that seemed in favour of free trade and sound finance. Existing states such as Turkey, Morocco, and Zanzibar were strengthened as long as they provided a framework for British trade. On the 'tribal frontiers' of the world this policy broke down; tribal authority could not offer the necessary guarantees to trade and investment. One alternative was to encourage white settlement. European colonization on the tribal frontier would create new markets. It would also result in the setting up of stable, self-governing white communities who would treat British merchants fairly. They would themselves pay for the expense of maintaining law and order. A second alternative was to work through chartered companies, private concerns that would shoulder the risks and expense of colonization. Chartered companies were not always practicable, and direct imperial intervention remained as an unpleasant but sometimes unavoidable expedient.*

In Africa direct British occupation gathered momentum as other European states began to expand their influence. Alien colonization was not regarded as dangerous to British interests as long as foreigners were willing to admit British merchandise and investments on the same terms as those of their own citizens. This expansion, however, became a more serious matter when British industries declined as a result of other European industrial nations raising protectionist tariffs. Britain was unwilling to break with free-trade policies, or to reimpose the hated food taxes that were bitterly unpopular among urban employers and employees alike. Imperialists argued that Britain should not stand aloof from the scramble for Africa lest the nation one day find itself excluded from valuable potential markets. More colonies were needed if only

* See also J. Gallagher and R. Robinson, 'The Imperialism of Free Trade', in *Economic History Review*, 2nd Series, vol. VI, 1953, pp. 1-15.

as some kind of an economic insurance policy. Africa might be an unprofitable field of investment at the moment, but its future potentialities should not be neglected.

Late nineteenth-century colonization on the Dark Continent was not, therefore, as has been argued by Hobson and Lenin, merely the result of an increasing British tendency to export capital, the product of capitalism in its last stage of development. For one thing, the importance of Africa as a field of British investment was very small when compared with countries such as North and South America, which absorbed vast British loans throughout the nineteenth century without necessarily becoming the object of interventionist policies. In Africa, moreover, capital exports did not always lead to expansionist policies. The founding of the Standard Bank of South Africa in 1862 was an important event in both British and South African economic history. This was one of the first banks to be set up on the basis of recent British joint stock banking legislation. The bank began when capital was plentiful on the London market, and when a great many similar institutions were being formed overseas with the help of British capital; yet at this period there was no desire in England to pursue an active imperial policy – despite the pressure of capital available for export.

British expansion in Africa was more a reaction to the policies of other European powers, as well as to the challenges set up by the particular local conditions encountered on the frontiers of South Africa, than the result of imperialist greed for colonies. It would be a mistake, too, to imagine that the imperialists had things all their own way even in the heyday of African empire-building. Expansion was then hardly ever opposed on the grounds that it was better to leave primitive races to their own devices; few nineteenth-century Europeans or Americans doubted that white rule was better than any kind of rule indigenous tribes might set up. The demand for imperial intervention, for redcoats and gunboats, often came from missionaries and humanitarians, while hardheaded business men frequently stood aloof. The arguments advanced against imperialism were in fact of a severely practical kind. The British Treasury was always afraid of incurring more expense. The British taxpayers usually objected to financing colonization, except when passions were stirred. The more cautious diplomatists feared that colonization might lead to disturbances in the balance of power or even to war. Great Britain in the end was nevertheless drawn into the African maelstrom and added a vast, though relatively short-lived African empire to her possessions.

One of the keys to the continent was Egypt. Turkish power, once supreme over the country, was visibly declining. The 'Sick Man of Europe' no longer seemed capable of keeping together his vast empire in Europe, the Near East, and Northern Africa. Egypt, meanwhile, was moving into the centre of the world's economic stage. The American Civil War led to a serious crisis in the vital textile industry; the interruption of transatlantic imports produced a great cotton famine. The valley of the Nile proved the ideal spot in which to grow cotton, and the Khedive Ismail, Egypt's ambitious ruler, attempted to modernize the country by using the proceeds of this most profitable cash-crop. Postal services, railways, lighthouses and military establishments were built; and, more important still, the construction of the Suez Canal was completed in 1869 with French help. In addition, Ismail endeavoured to pursue a policy of territorial expansion in Africa. The Khedive's plans were far too ambitious for his limited resources and for his inefficient administration. The peasants were squeezed dry by taxation. More and more foreign loans had to be taken up, and after the cotton boom collapsed, Ismail in 1875 was compelled to sell his shares in the Suez Canal to Great Britain. A year later he went bankrupt. France and Great Britain now assumed financial control over the country. Intervention led to an ineffective nationalist rising, headed by Egyptian Army officers, the country's Westernized military intelligentsia. In 1882 the nationalist forces were crushed by British troops at Tel-el-Kebir, and British influence became supreme in Egypt.

The Historical Background

The French, ousted from Egypt by the British, found some compensation in the Western Mediterranean and later in West Africa. Having established themselves in Algeria in 1830, the French regarded Tunisia as a natural adjunct to their possessions further west, even though the British and the Italians had some interests in the region. The French acquired a free hand in Tunisia in 1878 by acquiescing in the British occupation of Cyprus, which was designed to strengthen the British position in the Eastern Mediterranean and support the Turks against Russian pressure. In 1881 the French sent an army to Tunisia, and an active expansionist policy on the Upper Niger in West Africa followed.

The Italians were bitterly offended by the French advance, yet could not challenge their more powerful neighbour in the Mediterranean. Instead they looked for consolation elsewhere, and in 1882 occupied Assab on the Red Sea and established the colony of Eritrea, commanding the easiest approaches to the mountain kingdom of Abyssinia. Italy soon clashed with Abyssinia, which also coveted the seaboard. Abyssinia was the only indigenous African power successfully to participate in the scramble for Africa.

While the struggle for the northern portion of Africa was thus intimately linked to the conflicts among the more important European powers, the competition for Africa south of the Sahara was set off by a minor state. Leopold II, the King of the Belgians, took advantage of the growing interest of Western European traders and manufacturers in the potentialities of tropical Africa and the strong humanitarian feelings against the slave trade. A conference called in 1876 at Brussels discussed the best method of opening up the Dark Continent, and founded the International African Association. The Association, which soon became largely Belgian in character, sent Henry Morton Stanley in 1879 to the Congo as its agent. The drive for the Congo, another of the great gateways to Africa, was on. Belgian action stimulated French enterprise; by 1880 the French were pushing their claims on the Upper Congo.

The Portuguese, at first supported by the British, revived

43

old pretensions to the Congo. Rival claims were finally thrashed out at an international conference at Berlin during 1884–5. The Congo Free State was recognized by the United States and all the leading European powers as a sovereign body with the Belgian King at its head; various rules for the partition of Africa were laid down, and agreement was reached with regard to the suppression of the slave trade, and free navigation on the Niger and the Congo.

Congo diplomacy itself was closely linked to the wider problems of the balance of power in Europe. Bismarck, the most commanding figure on the Continent at that time, had little interest in African affairs. The Prussian landowners, whose interests he represented, were not after all concerned with palm trees in Little Popoland. Bismarck's primary aim in the field of foreign policy was to prevent the rise of an anti-German coalition that would challenge German continental supremacy. He sought to pursue this latter object by isolating France diplomatically, while at the same time encouraging her to seek compensation overseas for the loss of Alsace and Lorraine. He accordingly supported the French in Africa, and for a time even went as far as to associate Germany with France in a mildly anti-British policy of African colonization – a course that possessed the additional merit of being popular with Hamburg and Bremen merchants who had transmaritime interests.

Thus, for diplomatic rather more than for economic reasons, Germany joined the scramble. A protectorate in South West Africa was set up in 1884 and others followed in Togoland and the Cameroons on the West coast. A year later the Germans established themselves on the East coast in what is now Tanganyika, an area hitherto regarded as falling within the sphere of Britain. In 1886 the German colonial drive was called off. A great dispute had arisen between Russia and Austria-Hungary over the question of Bulgaria. Austria, Bismarck's ally, stood in need of British backing against Russia, and Bismarck, who considered Eastern Europe infinitely more important to Germany than the whole of Africa, began to adopt a much friendlier attitude towards Great Britain. The British, meanwhile, strengthened their neglected fleets and launched an effective counter-action on the continent of Africa.

THE BRITISH ADVANCE INLAND

Missions and commerce drew the British into the interior of East Africa but minerals were the attraction that drew white men in from the south. The advance of the miner's frontier inland from the Cape began in 1867, when diamonds were discovered near the Orange River. Prospectors of many nationalities flocked to the river diggings, but their finds were thrown into the shade when in 1870 diamonds were also found on the open veld. The tough frontier-town of Kimberley attracted pioneers from every part of South Africa, from Europe, and even from far-off Australia and North America. Economically the new discoveries meant that for the first time a vast amount of capital flowed into a region hitherto dependent on a few agricultural exports. It has been estimated by Professor S. H. Frankel, a distinguished economic historian, that 'the wealth accruing from the production of diamonds in South Africa has probably been greater than that which has ever been obtained from any other commodity in the same time anywhere in the world'.*

The precious stones were first secured by small entrepreneurs who practised open quarrying, but soon the old methods became inadequate. As mining operations became more complex and expensive, control over the industry was wrested from the small diggers by a few powerful companies. This process in turn led to centralized control, both of the South African diamond industry and of the diamond trade. Without monopolistic control the value of the diamond shares would probably have collapsed, as the result of overproduction or of catastrophic price fluctuations. So well did the diamond

* S. H. Frankel, *Capital Investment in Africa*, London (Oxford University Press), 1938.

producers succeed that they largely paid for the initial expansion of their industry from their own earnings. In addition, there was enough capital to finance further economic development elsewhere in Africa, in cooperation with investors from overseas, who mostly raised their funds in London. The chance for additional expansion came in 1886 when gold was discovered at the Witwatersrand in the Transvaal. Most of the concerns that were formed on the 'Rand' during its pioneering period were connected in some way with people prominent in the diamond industry.

The most outstanding of these financiers was an English parson's son, Cecil John Rhodes, who had come to South Africa for his health, and who became the greatest of the nineteenth-century Empire builders. In 1887 Rhodes acquired control over the whole of the De Beers mine at Kimberley; in the same year he also founded what later became the Consolidated Gold Fields of South Africa Limited. Rhodes's position on the Rand was not as strong as it was at Kimberley. But his great business achievements were regarded by Rhodes as mere stepping stones. The Rand, he was convinced, represented but a fraction of Southern Africa's mineral wealth, and some of the profits from the available mineral resources should be used to finance the exploitation of those additional reserves yet to be found inland. Rhodes linked the quest for minerals to further territorial expansion. He mistakenly imagined that a second Rand would be uncovered beyond the Limpopo River. Here, in what is now Southern Rhodesia, Rhodes's financial control would rule supreme, as it did not do in Johannesburg.

His guess at the time seemed by no means an unreasonable one. The far north was reputed to be the Biblical Ophir, the land of King Solomon's mines, and these speculations were confirmed by colourful and greatly exaggerated tales of the vast new gold deposits to be found inland, brought back by travellers such as Carl Mauch and Thomas Baines. Gold at this period was 'trumps', far more than it is today; for at the end of the last century most of the currencies of the countries engaged in world trade were still based on the gold standard.

Industry and commerce were expanding rapidly, but a good many years had passed since the last great gold discoveries in California and Australia had given a much needed stimulus to the world economy. Southern African gold was thus of key importance.

Rhodes did not think in economic terms alone. Inland expansion, he believed, would also lay the foundations of a new Empire that would one day stretch from the Cape to Cairo and rival the British Raj in India by its splendour. South African northward expansion would unite Briton and Boer in the common task of settling South Africa's half-empty hinterland, and bring civilization to the wide open frontier. Empire-building would also make the Cape, where Rhodes became Prime Minister in 1890, the gateway to the interior, and the most prominent state in Southern Africa. The Transvaal would be isolated, and later incorporated, together with the remaining South African colonies, into one united country, independent of direct British control, though linked to the British Empire.

To achieve these plans competition from Portugal and Germany had to be eliminated. First the Transvaalers had to be prevented from joining hands with the Germans in the interior, thus cutting off further advance from the south. Imperial intervention secured Bechuanaland, the 'Suez Canal into the interior'. Then, in 1888, Rhodes obtained by the Rudd concession a monopoly of all the minerals in the countries under the sway of Lobengula, the Matabele King. Rhodes amalgamated with various financial interests and, with the Matabele concession in his pocket, asked for a Royal Charter to secure powers of government north of the Limpopo River. The British Government of the day was little inclined to finance territorial expansion out of taxation, but had no objection if an association of private investors would shoulder the risks and expenses under imperial supervision. There was, after all, nothing to stop private entrepreneurs from 'going it alone' in the interior, and if colonization could not be avoided, it had best be carried on under official control.

White Settlers in Tropical Africa

A Charter was issued to the newly formed British South Africa Company in 1889. The following year Rhodes dispatched a small, but efficient, privately-paid and equipped force from South Africa, which successfully occupied Mashonaland. During the same period, rival trekkers from the Transvaal were firmly prevented from setting up any competing political authority beyond the Limpopo. President Kruger, the head of the Transvaal, cautiously decided not to intervene. In 1891, after lengthy negotiations, Rhodes's Charter was extended beyond the Zambezi up to the Congo, though the rich copper deposits of Katanga fell into Belgian hands. The foundations had been laid for permanent British settlement in Rhodesia.

In the meantime East Africa was being drawn into the sphere of British diplomacy. British influence inland depended to a considerable degree on the activities of British missionaries, who by the 1880s were established in Uganda and Tanganyika. In addition, John Kirk, the British representative accredited to the Sultan of Zanzibar, played an active part in protecting British interests. British persuasion had been effective in abolishing the transoceanic slave trade in Zanzibar. The Germans, however, concluded their first treaties on the East African coast in 1884, and German intervention made traditional British policy out of date. Two years later an agreement was signed between Britain and Germany whereby the two countries defined their respective spheres of influence in East Africa. The vast territory lying between the Mombasa coast and Lake Victoria was placed under the administration of the British East Africa Company, which after receiving a Charter in 1888 secured a precarious foothold in Uganda.

In Nyasaland, the situation was complicated by the ambitions of the Portuguese, who were now trying to make good their old claims to a great African empire stretching from coast to coast. The Portuguese plans met with bitter opposition on the part of British missionaries, traders, and planters in Nyasaland, who loathed the thought of being ruled by a Catholic

The Historical Background

Power, prone to protectionist policies, and with a bad record in the slave trade. Furthermore, the African Lakes Company, on which the Nyasaland missions depended for their supplies, found great difficulties in paying its way. Expenses were too high in relation to its small turnover; neither precious minerals nor gems were found to swell the Company's coffers.

Like other traders, the African Lakes Company soon discovered that almost the only legitimate merchandise which would stand the heavy cost of transport from the interior was ivory. To obtain this commodity, the Company extended its operations to the northern shores of Lake Nyasa, only to clash with Arab settlers who had established themselves politically and resented the Company's interference with their local monopoly. War broke out between the Muslims and the British traders; however, the Company proved incapable of driving the Mohammedans from their strongly fortified posts. Difficulties between the British and local Africans, especially the warlike Yao slave-traders, forced the British Government to take a more active interest in the handful of Europeans in the Nyasa country. Their numbers might be small, but they received powerful backing, especially from Scottish missionary societies and their lay supporters.

Active British intervention became a certainty when Rhodes offered financial assistance for a limited period to the British Government for the purpose of taking over Nyasaland for Britain. Rhodes's offer helped the British Government to send Sir Harry Johnston to Nyasaland, without having to apply to Parliament for funds, at a time when there was still a good deal of active opposition to further British expansion in Africa. Portugal was then forced to relinquish most of her claims, and her project of a great Central African empire was brought to an end. An amicable agreement was reached with Germany, now steering an anti-Russian and precariously Anglophile course. In 1890 the British position was recognized in Uganda, Kenya, Zanzibar, and on the western shores of Lake Nyasa, and by 1891 the whole of Nyasaland had become a British protectorate.

49

White Settlers in Tropical Africa

The British at first hoped to govern East Africa as they ran Rhodesia, by means of a chartered company, but the British East Africa Company lacked the vast financial resources which Rhodes was able to mobilize. Trade alone proved an inadequate base for the administration of a huge under-developed country. The Company managed to build a few warehouses at Mombasa, and opened an ivory caravan route to Uganda, but it could not make money. Between 1894 and 1895 a reluctant British Government was therefore forced to take over Uganda and British East Africa (Kenya), which became, like Nyasaland, protectorates under the administration, first of the Foreign and then of the Colonial Office.

CHANGING PATTERNS OF SETTLEMENT

The partition of Africa was decided overseas. Obviously, the local position in the various territories under review had some bearing on decisions arrived at by European statesmen in Berlin or London. The diplomatists usually had a good notion that certain tribes were more warlike than others, or that certain groups of white colonists, such as the British missionaries and traders established in Nyasaland, wielded a great deal of influence in England or Scotland. But on the whole, blacks and Europeans in Africa alike were looked upon in much the same way as the subjects of German princelings were regarded by eighteenth-century Cabinet diplomacy – as objects rather than subjects in the field of politics. This way of handling affairs at first worked pretty well, except in a few isolated cases, such as the Transvaal and Abyssinia, where the military potential of the local people was seriously underesti-mated. As far as actual settlement was concerned, however, the position was different; local factors were of much greater importance, and even the most self-confident planners soon had to adjust their ideas when brought face to face with the economic realities of Africa.

The Portuguese, the first whites in the field of settlement, had soon found this out. For several hundred years they had proved incapable of extending their effective influence beyond the coastal strips of the vast areas they claimed. Even the most daring expeditions inland, such as that made to Northern Rhodesia by a great Brazilian explorer and administrator, Francisco José de Lacerda, in 1798, had no long-term consequences. Individual Portuguese adventurers made their way into the interior, where they established semi-independent fiefs, some the size of an English county. Like feudal lords they lived in barbaric splendour, surrounded by bands of armed retainers and handsome black concubines, and dispensed their own justice. To their friends they offered regal hospitality; against their enemies, black or white, they waged war. The Portuguese Government lacked both the military and the administrative machinery to control these feudatories, or even to extract revenue from them. In the seventeenth century the Portuguese hit on an ingenious scheme. Large tracts of country were given away as *prazos da corôa* in return for an agreed annual payment and certain specified services. The grants were made for three lives on condition that the land would descend to the eldest daughters of the first and second proprietors. Men were required to marry Portuguese women born in Europe. The Portuguese in fact attempted to set up by law something like a matrilineal system of succession completely alien to their own social heritage.

This project to promote more effective control over the interior, and to encourage permanent white settlement, met with little success. Few Portuguese women were prepared to emigrate to fever-ridden East Africa; also the country probably lacked the economic resources necessary even for a centralized type of feudalism. The method of inheritance could not be enforced; many of the great estates passed into the hands of Goanese or mulattoes. The *prazos* themselves fell on evil days, partly as the result of disastrous native wars, and partly as the result of the slave trade – many *prazo* owners sold the tenants on whom their own economic prosperity and political influence depended. By the end of the nineteenth century the whole

51

economic outlook had changed in South-east Africa, and the *prazo* system went to pieces. The estates were controlled either by Portuguese military administrators, or by the officials of the Moçambique Company, a great commercial concern, strengthened by foreign capital, and endowed in 1891 with a Royal Charter.

In Rhodesia, the white warlords never had time to get firmly established, though they might well have done so in quite a number of areas had effective pacification been delayed. In North-eastern Rhodesia, for instance, an Englishman known to his African neighbours as Changa Changa carved out a little fief for himself, until his 'government' was brought to an end by the officials of the British South Africa Company. Another European, a German Jew by the name of Carl Wiese, became a well-known ivory-hunter and trader. He employed gangs of armed Africans and acquired considerable political influence in the Angoni country through various concessions from local chiefs. With the coming of the new order, Wiese lost his local political influence, disposed of his various grants and was forced to accept employment from a British concession company. Government now became a specialized function, exercised by salaried civil servants, and the régime of adventurers, a kind of 'bush feudalism', became a thing of the past in South-east Africa.

A very different way of life was led by the early missionaries, who were generally the first Europeans to take their wives into the inhospitable interior. Most Protestant missionary societies considered that the white woman had an essential part to play in the work of evangelization. A white man might convert a black man, but it needed a woman really to get to know the problems facing the African's wives and daughters. The white preachers also thought that the example of a white domestic household would be beneficial to African polygamists; the Protestant missionary authorities became convinced, moreover, that only the presence of his wife could prevent a missionary from falling into adultery and 'going native' in the conditions he then had to encounter.

52

The Historical Background

Coillard, who in 1877 set out on a great missionary expedition from Basutoland to the far-off Zambezi, a distance greater than that between London and Vienna, became a kind of ecclesiastical *voor-trekker*, a bearded patriarch, like the Boer. He travelled in great ox-waggons, accompanied by his wife and niece, his African evangelists and their families, his drivers and waggon-leaders. After he arrived at his destination, the early missionary had to do all the jobs of an ordinary settler – there were no shops inland. Transport was a major and sometimes an insuperable problem. The preacher also turned his hand to farming, to house-building, to medicine, and trade – in short he was a frontiersman. Mission work was frequently supported by laymen, Protestant artisan missionaries or Catholic lay brothers, skilled workers who were willing to accept poverty and even death in order to impart their skills to Africans.

Though the early missionary resembled the ordinary pioneer in many respects, there were two fundamental differences between himself and the settler. The missionary had a spiritual incentive and hoped to find the reward for his hardships in heaven, rather than in hard cash. His enterprise was moreover nearly always subsidized by others; Christian enthusiasts overseas contributed the funds which not only paid for the initial outlay required to set up stations but also helped to keep them going once they were established. The secular pioneer (with the exception of a few 'remittance men' sent overseas by wealthy families to get rid of them) had to find his own capital and had to keep himself going from the proceeds of his own efforts. Missionary settlement was not, therefore, a permanent solution from the economic point of view; the real work of transforming Africa's economy was effected through the profit motive.

In Rhodesia, minerals formed the first great incentive for immigration. 'Gold and the Gospel are fighting for the mastery,' wrote a Scottish missionary in 1889, 'and I fear gold will win.' His apprehensions were well founded. Rhodes occupied the interior by contracting with Major Frank William

Johnson for the organization, dispatch, and equipment of a pioneer column to Mashonaland. Johnson, an able man, half soldier, half entrepreneur, the sort of leader who would have gone far in Wallenstein's days, carried out his task quickly and efficiently. In 1890 a body of picked young men, accompanied by the British South Africa Company's own military police force, marched inland and hoisted the Union Jack where the city of Salisbury now stands.

The pioneers then disbanded to look for minerals, but the promised Rand could not be found. There were practically no alluvial gold deposits in Rhodesia – a heavy blow to many colonists, for only in its alluvial form could the gold be worked by men without capital. Transport proved a desperate problem, and mining was held back by the exceptionally onerous terms which the British South Africa Company initially imposed on the would-be miner. The pioneers suffered from hunger and disease; then war broke out with the Matabele in 1893. In a brilliant little campaign the colonists overthrew Lobengula's military oligarchy – a system of wage-labour defeated the raiding system. Three years later the Matabele took up arms once more and were soon joined by many of the Mashona tribes. Development came to a temporary standstill and many of the early settlers found themselves in desperate circumstances. Most pioneers were forced to sell their claims to their more fortunate compatriots who, like Johnson, possessed some liquid cash. Throughout the 1890s Rhodesia was a land of reckless speculation, carried on against a background of hardship and high expectation.

After the South African War, however, the mining industry was placed on a sounder footing. It was now clear that Southern Rhodesia did contain widely disseminated, low-grade ore bodies, which could be worked by syndicates of workers able to buy the required machinery. Mining remained a chancy business, and the names of many of the small Rhodesian mines read like *noms de plume* on today's lottery-tickets: 'Cross Your Luck', 'Clean Up', and 'Broke'.

The future lay with the big companies able to work at

greater depths and with enough capital to tide themselves over bad times. The small worker, nevertheless, played an important part in building up the country's gold-mining industry. Mining was encouraged by the discovery of vast coal deposits at Wankie, which did much to solve the industry's fuel problem, and by the building of an extensive railway network, which served the needs of the mining, rather than the farming industry. Other base minerals were found. Great impetus was given to mining in 1925 when it became clear that the enormous copper deposits south of Katanga (now known as the Northern Rhodesian Copper Belt) could be worked profitably, despite their low ore content. Rhodes's dream of a second Rand came true at last, and Northern Rhodesia became the land of giant mining concerns.

The early miner's frontier attracted a type of man very different from the man who went to East Africa. In Rhodesia all skilled work on the mines was done by Europeans who came from the Transvaal or further afield. White labourers were the only trained hands available. The mining townships and the little railway sidings also attracted white artisans, shopkeepers, and clerks, who did the jobs that in East Africa were then commonly done by Indian settlers. The unskilled work was left to Africans, tribal commuters, who worked in the European townships for a few months and then returned to their villages to farm in the traditional manner. The result of this combination of circumstances was that skin came to mark skill. The social structure of Rhodesia accordingly came to resemble that of South Africa or, in some ways, that of certain Eastern European countries where everybody was white, but where various immigrant groups, possessed of greater skill or more capital, had become superimposed on backward peasantries, without losing their ethnic identity.

The white miner or artisan in the early days had a difficult time. Whether he was a small entrepreneur or a salaried employee, he belonged to a labour force that was very unstable. His position resembled that of the black labour migrant, whose position was later investigated at considerable length by anthropologists and economists in Africa.* The European drifted from mine to mine and from job to job; he did not strike roots anywhere at first, for his permanent home lay outside Rhodesia. Many years passed before the immigrant came to look on a Southern Rhodesian town as 'home', the place where he meant to spend his old age as well as his working life. This stage had not yet been reached in the Northern Rhodesian mining townships. His position was in some respects even worse than the African's, for the white miner's rations and accommodation were not guaranteed to him.

Settled family life was rare at first. It was hard to bring up children in a colony where there were few schools, and where the breadwinner had to move about in search of work. Accommodation was poor, and drink, sport, gambling, and politics were almost the only kinds of entertainment available. Human life, moreover, was cheap. Not that early Rhodesia ever remotely resembled the Wild West or even Kimberley in their pioneering days of lawlessness. There were plenty of drunken pub-brawls, but no gunfights or stage-coach robberies; the early Rhodesian had a rifle to shoot game, but he never carried a revolver to protect himself. This was probably due to the fact that the country was reasonably well-policed from the beginning, and the British South Africa Company quickly set up an efficient, though relatively inexpensive administration. The social level was higher than was customary on other frontiers; there was a substantial number of younger sons of upper-middle-class families from Britain, though Rhodesia never remotely resembled the land of Eton boys and old Harrovians of colonial mythology.

* Observers of the disintegration of African tribal society have often blamed migratory labour for damaging tribal life. A modern anthropologist, W. Watson, in *Tribal Cohesion in a Money Economy*, Manchester (University Press), 1959, writing on the Mambwe of Northern Rhodesia, stresses that the loss of manpower to the village by labour migration does not necessarily injure tribal life. Whether it does, or does not, depends on the numbers that leave, on the family structure and economic set-up of the community in question. The Mambwe thus suffer little loss to their tribal life, but the Bemba do.

The Historical Background

The early settler's deadliest enemy was the malaria mosquito. Throughout the country's pioneering stage, white mortality was high; the building of the Beira railway especially cost a large number of lives. Conditions only began to improve just before the First World War, by which time the scourge of malaria was largely mastered. The national output increased, more capital was invested; more amenities and more social services were introduced; more families settled down to live in Rhodesia, and the proportion between men and women began to assume a more balanced appearance. Then, too, with greater specialization the white labour force became more settled and efficient, just as the African labour force was to become more stabilized, after a time-lag of well over a generation.

The European worker did not then consider, however, that there was any parallel between his own position and that of the African. The mines in Southern Rhodesia were much more scattered than they were on the Witwatersrand. The Rhodesian miners never achieved anything like the power and influence wielded by their colleagues down south. The Rhodesian miner was an individualist, like all the other settlers; he was moreover inclined to try his hand at many different jobs, often with the hope of becoming a small entrepreneur. He therefore felt an infinitely greater sympathy with his employer (a man of the same race and faith as himself, a man whom he might meet in the bar) than with the backward African labourer, whose ways were strange, and whose incompetence irritated him.

The gulf between white and black workers was further emphasized by sharp differences in their respective wages. Black, unskilled labour was relatively easy to get, once the pioneering period was over; it was cheap, although inefficient, as long as the African remained a commuter between township and kraal. But white, skilled labour could only be obtained at good wages; no one was willing to work in a colony where the cost of living was necessarily high, and where most of the amenities of older countries were lacking, unless he received a lot more money for it. The employers were on the whole quite

57

satisfied with this arrangement. It was obviously cheaper to employ skilled men who came voluntarily from elsewhere, than to train backward African villagers who were still tied to their old homes and way of life. Immigration, moreover, stimulated enterprise all around, by providing new markets and thus new opportunities, and constituting, as it were, the original pump-primer of the Rhodesian economy.

A number of unforeseen social difficulties arose. Africans slowly began to learn from their European workmates, and in some cases to compete with them, though mostly at lower wages. The less skilled Europeans especially began to resist this dilution of labour. They did so, not because they belonged to the 'kick-the-kaffir-up-the-backside' school of thought, as alleged by some of their critics, but for exactly the same reasons as many of their colleagues overseas resisted being underbid by women or by foreigners willing, or suspected of being willing, to work for less money. The real problem became that of closing the great wage-gap between skilled and unskilled labour. The task of improving the condition of the unskilled was complicated by the country's relative economic backwardness, and by the fact that the original scarcity of skilled labour had put up skilled wage levels to unaccustomed heights. The European workers argued that their stand was justified and that in the end it would benefit those Africans who did manage to gain entry into skilled or supervisory jobs. This contention acquired some point when, for instance, in 1959 skilled black workers in the Salisbury building trade began to complain of being undercut by white Portuguese labour migrants from Moçambique; so the problem was not destined to remain for ever one of white superiority.

The general economic balance sheet of white artisan immigration still remains to be struck. This is a difficult task, for there are many imponderables involved. A policy of encouraging the immigration of European workmen necessarily implied a high level of wages. Immigration of skilled men, just like any other kind of immigration, constituted a major social saving. For the new citizen brought something more valuable than just material goods; he also imported his own training and upbringing, permanent though intangible assets, produced at the expense of the immigrant's country of origin. Whatever the rights and wrongs of the controversy, the fact remained that Southern Rhodesia, which absorbed a relatively large number of white skilled workers, achieved a much higher level of economic diversification than all other countries between the Limpopo and the Sahara, yet its natural resources were much more limited than those of many other territories in the region.

The miner's frontier influenced farming in Rhodesia. The mines needed food for their white and black employees alike, as did the towns that sprang up in response to the needs of a mining economy. European agriculturists were attracted to the country and settled on the high veld, along the railway lines constructed to serve the miners' needs. Farming in Rhodesia was at first a scratch affair, for the British South Africa Company tended to give preference to big land companies in order to attract capital. Much land was, therefore, locked up in speculative ventures. Farming was further impeded by lack of markets; even though farmers could get both land and native cattle at very low prices, they found difficulties in making ends meet. The farmers frequently had to eke out their living by selling firewood, by transport-riding, or by prospecting. In addition, they had to shoulder all the experimental risks. A farmer might spend a great deal of money to improve his herds, only to have his beasts struck down by little-known cattle diseases. The properties of the soil were often unfamiliar, and again and again a farmer in Rhodesia or Kenya might lose all his capital.

Early farming was something of a gamble, like prospecting, and the man from overseas, unfamiliar with South African farming conditions, took an especially big risk. The history of Rhodesia's first Italian settlement bears this out. Between 1906 and 1908 a wealthy Italian army officer attempted to set up an Italian community in the Lomagundi district of Southern Rhodesia. Ten hard-working and experienced farmers arrived

59

from Italy, and the new colonists did all that the text-books said they should have done. By contemporary Rhodesian standards they used intensive methods; they were able to spend a good deal of capital, advanced by their backer; they settled close to one another so as to be able to give each other help. But the scheme was a complete failure. There were financial complications and the perennial difficulty that their farms were situated too far from the nearest market. More important was the fact that their land, even though bought at only a few shillings per *morgen*, turned out to be over-valued. The soil was heavily mineralized, unsuitable for anything but stock-raising, a deficiency that none of the settlers knew about; Boer or British colonials with farming experience in the south did better.

Rhodesian farming methods gradually became more intensive. Just before the First World War the process was aided by the development of communications and the expansion of agricultural services in the Colony. Another great boon was the introduction of tobacco, a cash crop of relatively high value, limited in bulk, yet easy to transport. The agricultural and veterinary services available to farmers improved considerably. The introduction of motor transport after the war brought a social revolution to the countryside, greatly diminishing the farmer's former isolation; both goods and ideas could now move across Rhodesia with much greater speed. The huge farms of old were gradually subdivided; improved methods of cultivation and more machinery were employed; the use of labour became somewhat more efficient. The old-style farmer often gave way to a highly trained specialist, possessed of a diploma in agriculture or even an engineering qualification, who was able to repair the most complicated kinds of agricultural machinery himself.

More farmers came to the country, and many settlement schemes, such as the one undertaken after the Second World War at Karoi in Southern Rhodesia, proved highly successful. The pattern of agriculture began to resemble that of older countries overseas, though progress was still impeded by the fact that, except for cheap, unskilled labour, everything else, machinery, fertilizers, transport, repair services, was much more expensive for a Rhodesian or a Kenyan farmer than, say, for an American, working within the framework of a highly developed and integrated economy.

In East Africa, the pattern of land settlement took a somewhat different shape. When the Imperial Government became directly responsible for Kenya and Uganda, it was still faced with the problem of how to make control over the interior effective. British rule inland was difficult to achieve as long as all supplies had to be taken from the coast on the backs of African carriers, or as long as the slave trade continued unchecked. In 1895 a railway was started from Mombasa to the shores of Lake Victoria in the interior, for the purpose of destroying the traffic in slaves, advancing British influence, and opening a strategic back door to the still disputed Nile Valley. The railway, however, had to be paid for, and the British Government accordingly endorsed a recommendation made by Sir Charles Eliot, Her Majesty's Commissioner in East Africa, that Kenya's vast and almost empty highlands could in time become both a white man's country and an economic asset, and that the traffic derived from land settlement would make the railway a profitable undertaking.

Early in the twentieth century an active policy of colonization was undertaken. In making its decision, the British Government thought in economic rather than national terms; it was, in fact, so little concerned with the future national composition of the region that in 1903 it proposed to make a free grant of 5,000 acres to the Zionist movement, so that the Jews might set up a homeland of their own, with a Jewish Governor, though under British protection. The Zionists, however, refused the offer, with momentous consequences for the future, and the settlers came from Great Britain and South Africa.

The most outstanding of the new colonists was Baron Delamere, who had first visited the Kenya Highlands on a hunting trip. Delamere decided to settle in East Africa and returned there in 1903. He obtained a vast grant of land in the Njoro District and settled down to farm. Delamere's ideal was to transplant the social patterns of English country life, with its paternalistic relationship between gentry and labourers, to East Africa. But the reality turned out to be very different. First of all, there were enormous technical difficulties. Delamere, a man of outstanding ability, first tried to breed sheep; he imported rams to improve the local flocks, but his animals proved unsuitable. He then turned to cattle, but the beasts died. He next took to the cultivation of wheat, and inaugurated research in East Africa into rust-resistant varieties. After 1918 he returned to his ranch, where he eventually succeeded in breeding high-grade merino sheep. Delamere was not only the first European to experiment on a large scale in Kenya and to sink a great deal of capital, mostly borrowed, into the country, but he also became the political spokesman of the colonists, the foremost advocate of permanent European settlement, as opposed to colonization by planters, or managerial labour migrants who ran an estate in the colonies in order to retire to England in their old age.

Partly as the result of Delamere's efforts, a good many European settlers, many of them with aristocratic names, were attracted to East Africa. Their work resulted in the creation of an agricultural cash economy producing tropical crops such as coffee, tea, sisal, and pyrethrum. European settlement in Kenya was concentrated in the White Highlands, which were reserved for white colonists. In striking out for territorial segregation, the Kenya settlers, like their Rhodesian colleagues, were not necessarily guided by an unreasoning preference for light-pink as against dark-brown skin pigmentation. The old-style Rhodesian farmer, who was content just to grow a few patches of maize and keep some native cattle, was in fact rather pleased to have an African village or two near his farm, so as to be able to engage labourers more easily.

But once the farmer started to improve his methods and farm on somewhat more intensive lines, his outlook became much the same as that of the eighteenth-century enclosing

English landlord, who objected to the institution of the village common, and who would not suffer the villagers' small and diseased beasts to graze next to his own pedigree cattle. A backward, communal, agricultural economy could not easily coexist side by side with a more highly developed capitalist one, even if there had not been added difficulties of sharp difference in race, language, and custom between the two races. Territorial segregation became the order of the day in Kenya as it did in Southern Rhodesia and South Africa.

A certain amount of white colonization took place further to the south along the East African plateau. In Tanganyika, the Germans encouraged European farming, but land settlement there was never as close as in Kenya. After the First World War, many of the German farms passed into the hands of British, Greek, and Indian purchasers, so that the character of settlement has become far more cosmopolitan than in Kenya. The settlers were much fewer in number and their farms more closely intermingled with African holdings than to the north. Tanganyika's political future under the British mandate seemed insecure to many prospective settlers, so that the whites in Tanganyika never attained anything like the influence which they managed to build up in Kenya. Nyasaland likewise attracted only a small number of settlers, mostly planters who grew coffee, and later tea, tobacco, and other crops, but whose general political and social influence remained limited.

The general pattern of settlement in East Africa has been rather different from that prevalent in most of Rhodesia. In the former region, the European community consisted in the main of planters, civil servants, and the employees of trading and land companies, a large proportion of whom formerly retired to England at the end of their working lives in the same way as did most British people settled in India or Ceylon. Rhodesia, on the other hand, is rather more like South Africa; the country possesses a substantial European working class, and many white traders and clerks, who do the jobs that frequently may be done by Indians in East Africa. Rhodesian society lacks that upper-middle-class character on which many Kenyans pride themselves; and the general social difference has become even more marked since secondary industries have begun to make their appearance in Southern Rhodesia.*

Rhodesian economic development resembled that of other settler countries overseas such as Canada, Australia, and even the United States, which financed their initial development and immigration by the development of a variety of foodstuffs and other raw materials for export to the world markets. In every one of these countries, the development of secondary industry came as a later step, and the same was true in Southern Rhodesia, now the most advanced of the African territories under consideration. The country's early secondary industries arose from the processing of local agricultural products such as cheese and bacon; all additional requirements had to be imported. During the Second World War, however, Rhodesia was largely cut off from overseas supplies, and the country's infant industries suddenly enjoyed a degree of protection which their competitors in the most autarky-minded countries might have envied. Production increased, especially after the war.

Important economic landmarks were the installation of a valuable cotton-spinning mill in Gatooma in 1943, and the opening of a large iron and steel works at Que Que five years later. Bulawayo and Salisbury have become manufacturing towns of some importance. Expansion was facilitated, not only by the country's ability to import capital from overseas, but

* Northern Rhodesian civil servants now also tend to be drawn into Rhodesian society despite the Southern Rhodesian stereotype of the 'fly-by-night' official, who goes to Fiji one day and to Honduras the next. The majority of civil servants in Northern Rhodesia stay in Rhodesia all their lives; many of them want to retire there, and they have their children at school there. They are known locally and know local conditions. If they want to supplement the dwindling value of their pensions they can get jobs locally. The English attitude, 'too old at forty', does not apply to the same extent. It is also not regarded as shameful for a senior civil servant on pension to come back to work as a junior clerk, as it would be in England.

also by the willingness of many technicians, specialists, and managerial experts to settle down permanently in Rhodesia. The country's economic progress in fact became one of the fastest ever attained in the world. Development in turn created many new social problems which Rhodesia shares with other industrial countries, but which have become further emphasized by the fact that the differences in income, education, and social background that exist elsewhere between managers, technicians, and foremen on the one hand, and the unskilled and semi-skilled workers on the other, often correspond to differences in colour.

While development in Angola and Moçambique has not kept pace with that in the Federation or the ex-Belgian Congo, it has, by Portuguese standards, been remarkable. President Salazar began in the 1930s to make up for centuries of neglect and maladministration. Immigration was encouraged, provincial budgets were balanced, and capital was found to stimulate economic growth. The white population of Angola in 1940 was 44,000, in 1953 it was 110,000, and by 1961 it was estimated at nearly 200,000. Moçambique in 1940 had 27,500 whites; in 1957 it had over 80,000.* A greater number of settlers go to Angola because the administration is more willing to accept poor peasants, whereas Moçambique insists on skilled workers. Still Portugal lacks sufficient resources to develop its colonies and fear of letting in foreign business groups has impeded development. The major development schemes involve irrigation, hydro-electric power and agricultural settlement. In Mocambique it is the Limpopo Valley Immigration Project which is opening up land for white peasant farmers. In the southern part of Angola in the Cela region, two large agricultural colonies are being established.

In contrast to the ex-Belgian Congo, where the white population is almost entirely limited to technicians, businessmen, and civil servants, Angola has fewer technicians but a large agricultural peasant class. Moçambique is more like Rhodesia

* For more detailed figures of white settlement in these and the other countries referred to, see Appendix, p. 159ff.

65

in its population structure, but with a much smaller engineer-technician class.

The Portuguese view Angola and Moçambique as agricultural provinces. Starting in the 1940s with the Huíla plateau project and increasingly since 1950, Lisbon has been trying to recreate Portuguese life in Africa by establishing peasant farming communities. No African labour is allowed; the white man must work as he did in Portugal. While friction is avoided in this field, Africans are becoming resentful of the competition of semi-skilled white labour, cutting them off from jobs and opportunities they formerly had. Furthermore, money diverted to preparing European *colonatos*, or village settlements, leaves less for African welfare. *

---

* The 1957 budget of Angola called for an expenditure of 140,000 dollars on African housing, the same amount as was spent on public monuments. See J. Duffy, *Portuguese Africa*, Harvard (University Press), 1959, p. 331.

Chapter 2

PATTERNS IN WHITE AND BLACK

THE effect of European immigration has been sharply to stimulate economic development and also to superimpose a new racial group on Africa's black inhabitants. In this respect South and East Africa might be compared with Eastern Europe in the Middle Ages, which also attracted many foreign colonists – Germans, Jews, and others. These immigrants came in numerous different capacities, as landowners or administrators, as traders or money-lenders, craftsmen or farmers. The newcomers were often responsible for founding the new towns, and their interests frequently began to clash with those of the original peasant peoples who remained entrenched in the country-side without generally absorbing the immigrants. Strife between the different ethnic communities usually became accentuated in the nineteenth century when economic development quickened; the towns grew apace, and more and more peasant lads migrated to the once alien or half-alien cities to seek their fortune. Immigration from the country-side often changed the national character of the townships, whilst mass education led to the emergence of indigenous, peasant-bred intellectuals who often became the standard bearers of a new nationalism, bitterly hostile to their minorities.

A comparable development is now beginning to get under way in parts of Southern and Eastern Africa; some of the problems familiar to Eastern Europe are turning up in a new dress, and new nations are being born. What then is a nation? A cynic once defined it as a group of people who live in the same country, believe the same lies about their ancestors, and hate their neighbours with the same intensity! He overstated his case, but a sentiment of nationalism cannot arise without a territorial focus, a feeling for a shared past and a common future, and a sense of being different from surrounding groups.

67

White Settlers in Tropical Africa

In today's multi-racial Africa, few nations in the Western sense have as yet arisen; they are still in the making. In this respect there is much similarity between whites and blacks in Africa. In a purely African setting, black men more often than not think of themselves in terms of tribal affiliations such as Zulu, Ngoni, or Bemba. When face to face with the whites, they speak of themselves as Africans. In a different social context, they may emphasize their home territory and describe themselves as Ghanaians, Nigerians, or Nyasalanders, even though the political units to which they refer were at first nothing but artificial creations, reflections of the balance of power as it existed among the European imperial powers at the end of the last century.

Europeans in Black Africa speak of themselves as English, Portuguese, or Afrikaners. Sometimes they refer to themselves as whites, and sometimes, when in conflict with pressure groups from overseas, as Rhodesians or Kenyans. With the exception of the Afrikaners in South Africa, no European community in Africa has developed a language of its own, nor is it likely to do so. Again with the exception of the Afrikaners, no white group in Africa has as yet produced any original kind of art; and though the level of cultural interest has been rising rapidly in recent years, the colonists' cultural life is still derivative, and centres on London or Lisbon rather than Beira or Bulawayo.

Migration, nevertheless, has produced new loyalties and new traditions. New communities have come into existence, and it is possible to see cases of 'proto-nationalities' – groups of people moving slowly towards nationhood. The most obvious factor in the making of a 'proto-nationality' is length of residence. Labour migrants, white or black, regard themselves as bound to the land of their origin until they become definitely settled in the new country. Rhodesians, most of whom are now permanent residents in the country of their birth or adoption, have a greater sense of belonging than Belgian Congolese, the majority of whom expect to return to Brussels when their contracts have expired. Portuguese peasants brought in to settle the Huíla region regard themselves as Angolans; emotional ties as well as those of self-interest now permanently link them to their new homes.

Another factor tending to unite the whites is a common feeling of having to stand together against the blacks. While whites may sometimes be divided amongst each other on national lines (Southern Rhodesia, for example, contains a considerable Afrikaans-speaking minority in addition to significant numbers of Greeks, Portuguese, Hollanders, Jews, and other national groups), these differences dwindle away when confronted by African nationalism. The whites, however poor they may be, mostly have comparable standards of living to maintain.* None of them would be willing to exist on an African level of subsistence. They all have comparable traditions of religion, education, and behaviour. They all adhere to the Western tradition of monogamy. They believe that their ways are not just different but morally superior to those of the indigenous Africans.

The Europeans, moreover, are held together by a feeling of having to join in defence of their political and social interests; in this respect, religion seems to make little difference, and the feelings of a Portuguese Catholic in Lourenço Marques are remarkably like those of a British Protestant in Umtali. Colonists are divided by differences of social class, but these are not now sufficiently marked to cut off white from white. There is little chance at present of the European working class combining with the black proletariat against their employers, for it is precisely the most poorly-paid European who regards himself as most severely threatened by African advancement.† His problem, like that of a low-paid African clerk, is also, to some extent, a psychological one. Men in well-paid positions with an assured place in society can afford to be egalitarian,

---

* There is some class snobbery in Rhodesia, and income levels are fairly stratified. All the same, Rhodesia is more egalitarian than England.

† The bitter inter-white class warfare that shook Johannesburg in 1922 (at that time the Africans stood passively aloof) is not likely to recur.

without losing caste. Insecurely placed groups, on the other hand, tend to make fine distinctions. It is for this reason that a European artisan will sometimes stress his status as a white man and refuse to shake hands with an African doctor, while an African clerk will similarly often stress his status as a white-collar worker and refuse to do manual labour.

The colonist's attitude is also affected by the conservatism that characterizes any immigrant community which is doing reasonably well for itself. This applies to colonists in Rhodesia as much as in Wisconsin and has little to do with either racialism or personality. Most immigrants, except for a small number driven out by political or religious persecution, leave home for one reason only – to gain a better chance in life. Provided they can better themselves and make money, they are not interested in political changes. Contrary to the old American right-wing stereotype of the alien with a bomb in his pocket, it is the new colonist who tends to accept things as they are; and it is the stay-at-home who is often a radical.

The featureless quality of the social landscape also affects the immigrant's general social relations. The immigrant comes into a country where there are at first no relatives to help him out; there are no sisters and aunts to act as baby-sitters. His friends have been left at home.* In the new environment it is often the church which stands out as a natural social centre and provides fellowship for the uprooted. Religious communities – Lutheran, Greek Orthodox, or Dutch Reformed – can act as centres of national life without exciting the dislike usually accorded to minority political associations. But churches are limited in their impact on the racial situation; however fervently they may express the ideals of racial equality and human brotherhood, however sincerely they

* To some extent, this tendency is counteracted by what might be called 'nuclearization'. The immigrant writes home to his friends and relatives that he has come to a good country. After some time he is joined by a brother or a friend from home. This explains the creation of small groups all hailing from the same region, such as the Sephardic Jewish community in Southern Rhodesia, who came from the island of Rhodes, or an early Scottish group who came from Lanark.

attempt to create a non-racial community, white and black congregations usually follow separate ways.

The general social position is further affected by broader factors. The Portuguese who colonized Brazil during the course of the seventeenth century were still a rural people; they did not differ nearly as much from their Negro African slaves as did nineteenth-century British emigrants from the indigenous people they found. Drawn from highly industrialized cities, the British settlers clashed with Matabele tribal warriors in 1893, when the gap between Europe and the remainder of the 'underdeveloped' world had immeasurably widened. The Negro and the Indian, moreover, were to some extent absorbed by a new Portuguese culture in tropical Brazil. The British in Rhodesia or Kenya, the Portuguese in Angola or Moçambique, were never numerous or brutal enough to crush the tribal systems of the indigenous people. The African tribes retained their languages and most of their social cohesion. Their position never resembled that of the Negro slaves who were brought to Brazil, the West Indies, or Alabama. The linguistic and cultural traditions of the slaves were completely smashed, with the result that they more easily became assimilated to the culture of their masters. Neither did the indigenous Africans suffer the fate of the American Indians or the Bushmen. The Bantu were a vigorous people, sufficiently advanced in technology to have reached the Iron Age; they managed to adapt themselves to the new economy in a way scattered groups of hunters and food-gatherers did not.

The Bantu tribal system continued to exist side by side with the much less numerous white society, with little merging between the two. In this respect, Southern and Eastern Africa again sharply differed from a country such as Brazil. The Portuguese who made their way overseas in the sixteenth and seventeenth centuries were mostly unmarried men. Only a few white women emigrated, and many Portuguese entered into liaisons or marriages with coloured women. In Rhodesia, the situation was different. During the pioneering days, affairs between white men and black women were admittedly quite common, but soon the position changed. Vast improvements in transport facilities and conditions of health brought European women in growing numbers. As soon as they arrived, they began to enforce a rigid colour bar in the sexual sphere.* The same process is now at work in Portuguese East Africa, where Portuguese women are insisting on standards very similar to those demanded by their British sisters. Miscegenation is accordingly decreasing rather than increasing; those who will not conform are looked upon as eccentrics at best or perverts at worst.

Settler cohesion is also solidified by pressure from outside. The Ngoni tribesman, like the Arab Bedouin, may appear as a fine or romantic figure to the European in a highly-developed and prosperous country, where there are no serious minority problems. But the attitude of a European surrounded by primitive tribesmen and a much smaller number of half-educated and educated Africans is understandably different. The British colonist in Rhodesia, or for that matter the Jewish settler in Palestine, does not feel the same way about his African or Arab neighbour. Whatever anthropologists or historians may tell him about cultural relativism, he is convinced that his is a better way of life, and he means to maintain it as he thinks fit. The colonist's reaction may be criticized; it is in itself neither especially noble nor ignoble but the consequence of a given social situation. Scathing condemnations from metropolitan critics, sometimes misinformed or unrealistic in character, do not improve the situation. The settlers resent interference from outsiders, who do not themselves have to bear the cost of or accept the consequences of the policies which they advocate.†

The colonist, like the African, believes, not always without justification, that the interests of his territory are liable at

* Legislation was passed in Southern Rhodesia in 1903 forbidding intercourse between black men and white women, but women's pressure groups failed to get a similar law passed forbidding intercourse between white men and black women.

†However, settlers often expect the metropolitan country to bear the responsibility for local white policies – for example, in Kenya and Algeria.

times to be sacrificed to those of the mother country. The settlers of Lourenço Marques or the Africans of Lusaka both often feel that their interests suffer through government by remote control; the fact that the settlers often have serious misconceptions about the way the state machinery works does not improve the situation. In Rhodesia this feeling makes for increased attachment to locally-based institutions. In the Portuguese colonies, with their rigidly centralist tradition, European separatism is denied any open outlet, being regarded as a serious political offence; but separatism continues to exist, nevertheless, even though it may have been driven underground.

The new colonist comes into a vast and almost empty country. The bureaucratic network is comparatively small; more is left to the individual's initiative. Whether a man is a farmer or an archivist, he has to tackle a wider range of tasks than he would have to do in a comparable job at home. Rapid economic and administrative expansion, moreover, have worked like a suction pump. The position is comparable to that which arose during the French Revolution, where the rapid growth of the armed forces permitted speedy advancement from the existing cadres of officers and N.C.O.s.

The old class divisions of the metropolitan countries no longer play the same part. Businessmen and mechanics may now live on the same road on plots originally bought as a speculation. Differences in status are evened out and the main criteria of social prestige that remain are essentially those of income or professional success. These attitudes are characteristic of all settler countries; they correspond exactly to what many nineteenth-century travellers found in the United States and New Zealand. To some extent, they are also common among the black migrants to the new towns – in Salisbury or Bulawayo it no longer matters whether a man belongs to the highly aristocratic Crocodile Clan from Bembaland or whether he does not.

The European immigrant community is also distinguished by certain demographic features. White Rhodesians, for instance, form a very youthful group; older people do not often go overseas, and the number of elderly persons in Rhodesia, small in itself, is further diminished by the fact that a good many pensioners retire to the Cape or elsewhere. Since a youthful population has more children than an ageing one, the settler birth rate is very high.* A high birth rate and a low death rate considerably affect the general settler outlook on life. There is also a high divorce rate in Rhodesia, exceeded only by that of the United States and Israel. The prevalence of divorce itself reflects the instability brought about by migration and by the relative absence of family ties; there are few 'grannies' about to give advice or to help with the family, and young parents meet with more difficulties than they would at home. A good deal of money is spent on sports and entertainment; Rhodesia, after all, possesses a splendid climate but few libraries and no permanent professional theatres or opera houses, so that people have to devise their own entertainment to a much greater extent.

The European communities are also asserting their separateness by creating their own culture-heroes. To Kenyans, Lord Delamere represents the struggles and achievements of British settlers under difficult circumstances. The Allan Wilson Patrol, massacred after an heroic fight during the Matabele War in 1893, stands for many Rhodesians as a 'symbol for the heroic few among the barbarous many, for the supremacy of the white man's spirit even in death'.†

Post-war immigration into Southern Rhodesia has swamped the pre-war generation of Rhodesians. Descent from a member of the Pioneer Column, formerly endowed with a quasi-'Mayflower' prestige, is no longer recognized as an honour by the new men. The more recent settler tends to be more pragmatic

* Between 1956 and 1958 the European rate of natural increase fluctuated between 2.1 and 2.3 per cent per annum, which is one of the highest white reproduction rates in the world.

† P. Mason, *The Birth of a Dilemma: The Conquest and Settlement of Rhodesia*, London (Oxford University Press), 1958, p. 181. For a romanticized account of the Wilson Patrol, see A. Fullerton, *The White Men Sang*, London (Peter Davies), 1958.

and less interested in his country's history. He is, moreover, endowed with a relatively high degree of self-confidence *vis à vis* the older Rhodesian, a factor which differentiates Rhodesia to some extent from older countries of settlement. The new Rhodesian, unlike the mass of Polish or Irish immigrants who came to America in the last century, is not necessarily poorer or less well educated than the people of his new country. Most of the new colonists come from English-speaking countries and therefore have no language problem to hold them back. And the foreign immigrant is not under the same compulsion to assimilate as he was in the United States. Rhodesia in this respect is more like South Africa or Canada, where cultural pluralism is an accepted fact.

Immigration establishes new loyalties. The settler community is still relatively small, and though life is getting more impersonal in a big centre like Salisbury, no settler country as yet knows the 'lonely crowd' of the older countries overseas. The pressures that make for social cohesion are much stronger than those that work against it; the result is a relatively high degree of community integration.

The new solidarity is symbolized by a new kind of speech. Rhodesia is the only African settler country outside South Africa to have produced an accent of its own, a phonetic amalgam compounded of Afrikaans, Scottish, and Cockney elements. The importance of the new accent is hard to exaggerate. For whatever the parents may have spoken, German or Spanish, B.B.C. or Lancashire, the Rhodesian school child picks up the new speech, which, like the Australian or American accent, evens out older class and national divisions, and marks off the 'Ridgebacks', the born Rhodesians, as a recognizable group apart. The fate of the new proto-nationalities will not, however, be decided in isolation. Whatever happens, the Europeans in tropical Africa will remain minorities; their future is indissolubly linked with problems of race.

The term 'race relations' is unfortunately used very loosely. Race itself is a biological concept which assumes that people are distinct from one another and that they have hereditary differences. Yet the concept of race is not agreed on by scientists, whose use of the term differs greatly from that of laymen. Race has now come to have a sociological meaning – it means a group of people who are set apart as if they were a race. Race relations and race attitudes to some extent flow from this fact of easy identification. Thinking that people are different makes it easier to develop fixed attitudes towards them.

But is there such a thing as 'race relations'? Its study sometimes seems like that of international relations, arbitrarily cut out of history. Race relations are not a unique kind of social contact; they embrace all kinds of ways, economic, political, ideological, in which people either do or do not get on with each other. The manner in which they are shaped depends on the general social environment, and is itself strongly influenced by economic factors.

The extreme vanguard of European settlement was formed by elephant hunters and ivory traders, like George Westbeech in Barotseland or Carl Wiese among the Ngoni. The ivory hunter, like the French-Canadian fur trapper, was the only European whose activities fitted relatively easily into the African tribal structure; race relations between these early frontiersmen and, say, Matabele chieftains, were thus rather egalitarian in character. Both groups needed one another and looked upon their opposite numbers as what they were, an armed aristocracy whom it was necessary to conciliate.

Ivory, however, was not an inexhaustible source of wealth. Gradually the elephants were shot out, and new kinds of wealth had to be found. After Africa was conquered, different kinds of economies were built up, economies that depended on the export of primary products like maize, tea, coffee, copper, gold, and diamonds for the world market. The European came in as entrepreneur and supervisor; the African became the unskilled labourer, who had to be prised out of his tribal environment by all kinds of pressure. The tribesman straight from the kraal was an inefficient labourer, and the position was made worse by the wasteful use of labour by many

Europeans. Race attitudes were accordingly determined by
the attitude of the supervisor towards poorly paid and unreliable hands.

Power and domination, moreover, had a profound effect on
many whites. The officials, though paternalistic and often
sympathetic in their attitude, were ruling a people no longer
bound by the same restraints as of old. They became convinced that firmness was the only answer. Isolated employers
of hundreds of Africans on lonely mines and farms adopted
similar ways, for otherwise they could hardly have carried on.
The kind of social tensions that appeared on a Rhodesian farm
were in fact similar, to some extent, to those in England during
the period of high farming in the nineteenth century. Wiltshire
labourers in the seventies were in a position comparable to
that of Rhodesian labourers seventy or eighty years later. The
English labourer's diet was monotonous, his housing was subsidized, wages were supplemented in kind by food and drink,
and the great landowners exercised a kind of patriarchal
supervision over their hands. Work was poorly paid, yet

those who are so ready to cast every blame upon the farmer and to
represent him as eating up the earnings of his men ... should remem-
ber that farming as a rule is carried on with a large amount of borrowed capital ... the slightest derangement of calculation in the
price of wool, meat, or corn seriously interferes with a fair return ...
the farmer has to sail extremely closely to the wind.

From the labourers' point of view, of course, things appeared
in a very different light and their betters concluded that

they are too ungrateful for the many great benefits which are bounti-
fully supplied to them – the brandy, the soup, and the fresh meat
readily extended without stint from the farmer's home in sickness to
the cottage are too quickly forgotten.*

Kenyan and Rhodesian farmers felt exactly the same way, only
the gulf that separated them from their labourers was an even

* Letter by Richard Jefferies to *The Times* in 1872, quoted in full by
Bonham Carter, *The English Village*, Harmondsworth (Penguin Books),
1952, pp. 77–87.

greater one; and social, linguistic, and cultural differences were all identified with the one great bar of colour.

In a country where all unskilled labour was done by Africans, many whites developed 'a paralysing dependence on the Black, from that superior attitude that refuses to do this or that because it is kaffir's work, or feebler still, because the climate does not allow it'.* This point should not be overstressed. During the great slump, Rhodesian clerks and artisans were only too glad to work as navvies making roads, and status considerations ceased to count. But, generally speaking, the presence of cheap though inefficient black labour had a bad effect on some people – it deadened their initiative and robbed them of the challenge to invent in order to compensate for that shortage of labour which drove the whites on the United States frontier to experimentation and innovation.

Most settlers who wanted to emigrate did not choose to come to Africa in order to satisfy hidden desires to dominate the inhabitants, but simply as a result of economic considerations or chance. All the same, some whites in Africa did gain a sense of power and of self-elevation as the result of African submissiveness, and this sometimes affected their attitude towards black men.† Social separation of the races was gradually emphasized by a conscious policy of segregation, which was built up into a theory of parallel development when the world slump hit Southern Rhodesia. Legal segregation found its clearest expression in the Land Apportionment Act of 1930, based on the idea that the town should belong to the whites and the reserve to the blacks.

Segregation, however, was not a simple matter but involved two contradictory aspects. On the one hand, it was looked upon as a protective device, and as such was supported by the British Colonial Office, by administrators like Lord Lugard,

* H. S. Keigwin, 'Segregation', in *Nada* (The Southern Rhodesian Native Affairs Department Annual), December 1924, p. 56.

† See D. C. Mannoni in *Psychologie de la colonisation*, Paris, 1950, for an exaggerated view of the psychological satisfaction whites gain from ruling Africans.

by convinced and ardent defenders of native interests such as the Rev. Arthur Shirley Cripps of Southern Rhodesia, as well as by the bulk of missionaries and native commissioners. Since the two peoples did not get on well together, it was argued, they should be insulated from each other. Unless this was done, the blacks would be exploited or debauched. Then there was the economic aspect. With almost no secondary industry and only a small white population, Rhodesia during the depression possessed neither the administrative machinery nor the material resources needed to care for a large number of Africans in the towns; in the reserves the Africans at least managed to keep alive on a system of subsistence agriculture. In addition, segregation was looked upon as a device to protect certain classes of Europeans. White artisans received some legal protection against being undercut by black labour. White farmers, like so many other producers all over the world, tried to 'feather-bed' themselves, at the expense of both the consumer and other producers, in this case Africans, operating with lower overheads.*

The economic effects of this policy are not easy to gauge. It is doubtful whether the Europeans themselves derived as much benefit from these restrictionist devices as they imagined. As far as the Africans were concerned, segregation of the kind current in Rhodesia in the thirties probably retarded development. Tribal backwardness remained as long as the reserves were inadequately serviced by roads or were left with inadequate agricultural and other technical services. Segregation of African locations in towns may also have helped to slow down the growth of a civilized urban class of Africans. Forced to live cheek by jowl with illiterate migrant labourers, African school teachers, traders, and clerks found it difficult to maintain the

* It should, however, be remembered that a great deal of development has taken place in the Southern Rhodesian reserves. Water supplies have been vastly extended; the pole-and-mud hut has mostly been replaced by brick buildings, whilst nearly 18,000 miles of roads are now being maintained by the Native Department. Development has been fastest near the towns, some reserves being found in the proximity of most Rhodesian settlements.

middle-class standards which the Europeans had taught them. The whites in their turn were often reinforced in their own sense of superiority by seeing the Africans live as they did, and their attitude again served to justify their demand both for continued separation and the need to retain control.

Segregation has produced various difficulties. There were, for instance, those of an ideological kind, for modern Europeans themselves argued that their conquest of Africa was justified, not merely on the grounds of superior force, but also because they came with a mission to civilize the blacks. The Transvaal Boers of old had not been confronted with this problem. They looked upon themselves as the Chosen People, and like the Hebrews wandered through a wilderness, threatened by a harsh climate, by the arrows of the Amalekites, by droughts and locusts, by disease and pestilence. Insecurity and danger moulded the trekkers into a solid group. Boer ideology was grim and harsh, but also egalitarian.

In the Cape, life was less austere. The Bantu problem was not so serious as it was in the north, there was more class differentiation, and attitudes towards the Africans were inclined to be more paternalistic. In the nineteenth century, moreover, the Cape attracted a good many missionaries who gradually began to convert large numbers of Africans. Christianity did not transform tribal Africans; they remained primitive. Christianity therefore ceased to be a passport to European civilization, and many whites argued that it was necessary to civilize as well as to Christianize Africans before they could be treated as equals.

In 1853 the Cape legislature passed a bill which gave the franchise to all British subjects, without distinction of race, on a limited property qualification. These qualifications remained until 1892, when fear about the numbers of Africans attaining the vote led to an increase in the property qualification and the institution of a simple education test. By 1898, the principle of 'equal rights for all civilized men' had spread to Southern Rhodesia, and a 'colour-blind' franchise was introduced for the newly-set-up legislative council. Although European opposition to any voting on the part of Africans remained strong, and the franchise qualifications were raised repeatedly for the purpose of keeping out Africans and poor whites, nevertheless the Cape – as opposed to the Transvaal – tradition was never fully renounced north of the Limpopo.

The criterion of civilization rather than colour became more important when Southern Rhodesia began to industrialize and found existing supplies of white labour inadequate. Secondary industry needed a more efficient labour force than the older mining and farming economy. After the Second World War Rhodesians, except for a limited number of conservatives, came to accept the need for a larger African work force in the towns. Few Rhodesians seriously advocated a policy of *apartheid* that would go hand in hand with the planned industrialization of the reserves, a much more costly policy. Industrialization was to centre on the towns where most of the required facilities were already in existence, and the need for ultimate assimilation became widely accepted as a necessary goal of policy.

Many Africans and some Europeans doubt whether there has in fact been a change; the new policy of partnership is therefore stigmatized by some as a trick designed to perpetuate white rule, or, at best, as an unconscious rationalization of white class interests. But the various shifts that have taken place in the European ideology since the twenties and thirties, when segregation was advocated by missionaries and negrophiles with the same fervour with which they now denounce it, cannot be interpreted in this simple fashion. These shifts did constitute a cautious response to a changing social situation, and have in turn helped to modify the social structure. This is true despite the fact that Europeans have also used their power in order to protect selected white groups, such as urban artisans, against lower-paid African competition.

European readjustment was a slow process. The Europeans were not always wrong in believing that even educated Africans often held on to standards very different from their own. The emigrant, for example, who had gone to Rhodesia from

England was a member of a small 'nuclear' family. He had recognized obligations towards his wife and children but not to cousins, nephews, or even parents-in-law, who usually lived thousands of miles away. Educated Africans were in a very different position. Clan and family loyalties pulled one way; loyalties to great impersonal organizations and the demands of an individual ethic pulled the other. If an African postal official refused to help his kinsmen in case of need, he would be called disloyal. If he favoured his kinsmen at the expense of the Posts and Telegraphs Department, the whites would call him corrupt. All too often, loyalty to kith and kin carried the day, but this naturally helped to determine the white man's attitude towards the black in a very unfavourable fashion.

The different pulls also made themselves felt in the ideological sphere. The newly-fledged intellectual was drawn one way by European rationalism and another by ancestral magic. Many highly-educated Africans continued to think in terms of magical beliefs, slightly adapted to a new social situation. Even today, many African schoolboys fear that their ball might be bewitched by the opposite team if their opponents get hold of it before a football match, while some African students continue to seek out the urban *nganga* (medicine man) for help in passing their examinations.

African intellectuals, like so many colonial, refugee, or minority intellectuals, are sometimes insecure and hypersensitive. They are 'wanderers between two worlds'. They often suspect insults where none are intended. Like most insecure refugees, they often hold two opposing but complementary stereotypes of the 'Establishment': the ruling class are moronic and stupid; they are terribly clever and their secret police force is omniscient. (This is rather like the Jews' stereotype of the Nazi ruling class.)

The African thrust into European society also had to adjust himself to a very different sense of time. If he was born in a village, he came from a background where there were neither clocks nor watches, nor was there any need for timepieces. There was a time for reaping and a time for sowing, but time was not·a commodity, capable of minute subdivision and endowed with monetary value. The average European, with his urban and industrial background, had a different sense of time, and readjustment for the African in his new milieu was no easier than for an eighteenth-century English peasant thrust into the mechanical discipline of a new factory. The European employer or supervisor was not interested in sociological explanations, and when the African did not conform to the European's time-sense he was called unpunctual or unreliable.

These objective factors apart, many Europeans were still very slow to recognize or give any credit to the fully emancipated African. The white men's reaction was to some extent affected by what might be called 'the law of the time lag'. All too often our notions of what other people are like are based on the real or supposed experiences of one's own group of a generation or two ago. The European stereotypes of Englishmen thus used to be based on impressions received from upper-middle-class travellers to the Continent in the nineteenth century. Stereotypes of the Jewish cloth pedlar or the fighting, drunken Irishman were based on impressions produced by immigrant Jewish textile workers and Irish navvies who settled in New York or London in the nineties. These stereotypes have persisted and still, to some extent, shape people's opinions about Jews and Irishmen, or for that matter, about white settlers in Africa, even though the original stereotypes were dangerous and misleading simplifications.

The European settler in Africa reacted in a similar fashion. Border clashes, cattle thefts, and periods of labour shortage earned the Bantu a reputation for violence, treachery, or laziness. These stereotypes continued even after great changes had taken place in the African social structure. They were intensified by social segregation, which often prevented the Europeans from meeting educated Africans. The white man's opinion of Africans tended to be based on his contacts with unskilled and poorly-educated labourers, on limited experience, and often on distorted history; but this the whites often failed to realize. Fear of the African's insanitary habits and the danger of diseases led to segregation in Rhodesian towns after 1908. The European's own eyes seemed to tell him that the African was inferior, that he was immoral, and that he needed firm handling. Admittedly the social roles and the prescribed behaviour between white and black were not fixed; they varied with the period of contact. Moreover, not all whites reacted in the same way; there were many gradations, ranging from outspoken and sometimes unbalanced Negrophiles, to the 'pukka sahib' type of military or administrative ruler, insistent on his own superiority, or the authoritarian personality who went out of his way to 'keep the kaffir down'.

The lack of social contacts, except those resting on an employer-supervisory basis, made it much more difficult for Rhodesians and Kenyans to perceive the differentiation taking place within African society or to meet the growing African middle class. In fact, though the cultural gap between white and black has been reduced, racial antipathies often remain; what usually happened was that the 'raw kaffir' of old became romanticized while the educated African, possessed of wider political aspirations than his backward brother in the village, became the main object of dislike for many Europeans. The advanced African often came to be regarded not only as a political danger but also as a threat to European status, for white status could no longer be assumed as an automatic right once Africans acquired degrees or became more than unskilled labourers.

The educated African was also affected by segregation. He too tended to form his own set of stereotypes, as far removed from the truth as the European's. Sometimes the white man became the arch-exploiter, infinitely clever and inspired by the worst of motives. The existence of a social and economic colour bar served as an excuse for those who would not have succeeded in their ambitions even in the most fully integrated kind of society. The black man's myth of the white also affected the lower strata of society. It became further distorted by blending with folk-myths of witches and vampire-men.

Patterns in White and Black

There is another side to it. The Federation and Kenya alike have made tremendous advances in agriculture, industry, education, and social welfare. A few steps have been taken to end some forms of social discrimination. But old attitudes persist, and the threat of personal insult, sometimes quite unintended, embitters many educated Africans. Social discrimination becomes all the more serious in Rhodesia as university-educated men are now accepted on equal terms in the civil service and are being recruited by some of the country's major firms. Rhodesia, furthermore, now aims at creating an African middle class to act as a buffer between the white *élite* and the black masses to solve the problem. But emergent middle classes in the past have often been the leaders of nationalist and revolutionary sentiment. The possibilities of further tension arising from economic competition must not be ignored. The British settler countries will thus still have to cope with major social and political problems even if they accept the educated African.

In both the Belgian and the Portuguese colonies, the situation is somewhat different. Neither the local whites nor the blacks have been running the country, since ultimate power has remained with the metropolitan country. Until recently only Belgian residents had representation on advisory councils. The Belgians effected great economic development in the Congo, and urban Africans enjoyed some of the highest wages paid out to black men in Africa. The Belgians encouraged the growth of an African skilled working class and lower middle class. By special decree in 1952, the *immatriculés* or *évolués* (the educated African *élite*) received almost the same status as a Belgian citizen. The Belgians, however, did not wish to joust with a university-trained *élite*. Africans formerly could not study abroad, and no higher education was given in the Congo until 1954.

Political rule in the Congo was based on a system in which the administration, a small group of interlocking companies and the Catholic Church formed a highly integrated centre of power. The bulk of the white people were migrants and the number of permanently-settled farmers small.* The Belgian community lacked that broader base of European artisans and clerks which formed so important a segment of the European population of Southern Rhodesia. African and European nationalists were discouraged; they could not move about freely nor rally support for their cause, and for a long time African opposition to the existing order was expressed in religious rather than political terms.

Then there was a sudden change in the approach from Brussels. Partly as the result of political shifts within Belgium itself, partly in consequence of severe rioting and intensive organization on the part of the Ba-Kongo majority round Leopoldville, the Belgians attempted to increase African participation in politics. Critics of the new course argued at the time that educated, urbanized Africans were not sufficiently strong in numbers to act as an effective counter-weight against tribalism, and that the government was acting too quickly in relaxing controls before a common loyalty to the new Congo state had been achieved, and before enough Africans had gained experience in posts of responsibility. These warnings were not, however, heeded, and the process of political reform quickly accelerated. The 1959 charter of liberties bred a multitude of parties and in the municipal elections there was a race among Congolese politicians to see who could demand the most. At the Round Table Conference of January 1960, all the African representatives demanded immediate independence. The Belgians were shocked to find that they had only two alternatives – to fight or to abdicate. Their authority and ability to maintain order had already gone. 'By the end of 1959 the position of the Belgians in the Lower Congo had grown almost hopeless. Their authority could be restored only by military force.'† With reason to fear that rebellion would break out elsewhere, involving a long guerrilla war, the Belgians chose to abdicate

* The number of *colons* or settlers in the Belgian Congo in 1958 was 9,621 out of a total European population of 109,457.

† See Colin Legum's excellent study, *Congo Disaster*, Harmondsworth (Penguin Books), 1961, p. 70.

and hoped that their generous attitude would save them.

The Provincial elections of 1960 were followed by an ineffective attempt in June to set up a national Congo government on parliamentary lines. The new government did not, however, prove capable of controlling the situation; the Force Publique mutinied; there were widespread disorders and intertribal clashes; Europeans were murdered, women raped, and many whites fled from the country. Central authority collapsed, and the relatively wealthy Katanga province attempted to secede from the new Congo state with Belgian backing. UN troops were then called in, from countries as different as Eire and Ghana, Sweden and Tunisia, to face the unenviable task of rebuilding a state-organization almost from scratch, but without a single national ideology to unite them. The Congo moreover was drawn into the whirlpool of the East-West conflict – with calamitous possibilities for the African future.

It is too early to evaluate what has happened in the Congo, but it is evident that the Belgians, who neglected political development for too long,. were caught unprepared by the rapid rise of Congolese nationalism. Although they are now attacked for running away, who would have supported Belgian resistance to the demands of the African nationalists? If the Belgians are to be censured for not training the Congolese in the arts of self-government, then the African leaders must also bear the blame for demanding immediate independence and for making a period of peaceful transition impossible.

The Portuguese, on the other hand, have continued to maintain their old imperial tradition. They insist that their overseas territories are provinces of Portugal – *Portugal do ultramar*; Portuguese, African, and Goanese civil servants are freely posted from one part of the empire to another, and thus retain a common interest in its integrity. Separatism is discouraged and authority is centralized in Lisbon, where the colonies are represented by eight deputies in the 120-strong National Assembly. The overseas population is divided into two classes – citizens and natives. The *indigenas* are the culturally backward people whom the Portuguese are trying to 'civilize'. Those Africans who have adopted the Portuguese language, religion, habits, and culture are called *assimilados* and qualify as citizens. They can become civil servants and are posted throughout the Portuguese Empire in a way in which British Africans never were, so that they have both a material and an ideological interest in thinking imperially rather than in terms of local separatism.

The Portuguese system, however, is not as stable as it once appeared. Few *indígenas* have attained the status of *assimilado* (3 per cent or 306,691 out of 10,000,000),* and many advanced Africans do not in fact wish to assume the full burdens of Portuguese citizenship. The *assimilado* is not always accepted as a Portuguese by his white compatriots. There is rigid police control of the *indígenas*; rebels or malcontents are exiled to offshore islands. Even more important is the fact that neither Angola nor Moçambique has as yet experienced the level of economic development that has brought such rapid social and political changes to neighbouring countries.

Historically, Portugal has always tended to limit outside investment, for the Portuguese have by bitter experience been made extremely wary of possible foreign claimants to their possessions. Yet Portugal lacks the resources to develop its colonies to the fullest extent of their potential. Development is slow and carefully controlled, while foreign enterprise is subject to a considerable degree of bureaucratic supervision. Even though economic enterprise has been rigidly supervised, the forces released may not be as easy to control as some Portuguese officials imagine. The thousands of young men travelling to the Rand or Rhodesia will pick up new ideas, and the influence of African nationalism in the Congo, Nyasaland, and Tanganyika will be hard to ignore.

The other danger is that the *assimilado* system itself is beginning to show some cracks. The Portuguese are assimilationist in theory, but even European foreigners who have become

* J. S. Coleman, 'Political Systems in Multi-racial Africa', in *Africa Special Report*, June 1958, vol. 3, No. 6.

naturalized Portuguese citizens are not always fully regarded as Portuguese. Minorities, such as the German farmers settled in Portuguese East Africa, do not merge into the Portuguese community, unlike their compatriots who settled across the border in Rhodesia and have quickly become Rhodesians. Many factors – the absence of schools, the lack of communications, differences of religion, etiquette, and language – affect the situation. All add up to the fact that the Portuguese are less assimilationist in practice than in theory. The black *assimilado* finds this out too; he enjoys full legal equality, but full social acceptance often eludes him.'

The Portuguese Government is sincere about integration, but the fact remains that the *assimilado* cannot always be found a proper job; economic development has not gone far enough to create opportunities for all the urbanized Africans who qualify for the higher status. The Government has thus decided to restrict entry to the *assimilado* class, partly, it has been argued, because this class of Africans was competing directly with established European artisans and semi-skilled workers. Rather than create trouble among *assimilados* (and whites), the governments of Angola and Moçambique seem to prefer to hold civilized Africans in the *indigena* class, which is more easily controlled by pass laws and labour contracts. As 'natives', they are thought to be less vulnerable to subversion or unemployment.

The qualifications for the *assimilados* have been raised.* An African must now be able to speak Portuguese 'correctly'. It is not enough for him to have abandoned native ways, he must also show that he has absorbed Portuguese 'civilization'. There are thousands of urban wage-earning Christian Africans who speak and write Portuguese but who are not *assimilados* – they are civilized *indigenas* who remain subject to all administrative controls.† This leads to a different kind of

* See *Estatuto dos Indígenas Portugueses das Provincias da Guiné, Angola e Moçambique* of 1954.

† See Dr M. Harris, 'The Assimilado System in Portuguese Mozambique', in *Africa Special Report*, November 1958, vol. 3, No. 11.

racial frustration from the one caused by Rhodesian practices, but it may be just as difficult to cure.

When the different territories under review are compared, it might seem at first sight that racial tensions seem greatest wherever there is a large settler class. It is true that competition between white and black for power and privileges does breed tension. Nevertheless, the conclusion mentioned above may well be based on an error of the *post hoc ergo propter hoc* variety. For it is precisely the multi-racial states that are undergoing the greatest economic development; and this creates new kinds of clashes, even though it also ultimately provides the physical means for resolving them. A kind of optical illusion is caused by the fact that in multi-racial territories those problems common to any rapidly developing country are seen quite literally in terms of black and white. The tensions of all-black countries in West Africa appear to be different; they are labelled class conflicts or seen as clashes between the urbanized and tribal *élites*. But fundamentally they are of a very similar order; once the Europeans in other parts of Africa find themselves in a position to remove the stigma of the colour bar, and once they permit their relations with Africans to be broken down into political, economic, and social components, they may find a change of atmosphere.

A new approach towards the emergent African *élite* may thus pay the Europeans better than any other kind of policy, even though it may involve many difficulties. As far as the details regarding the distribution of political power are concerned, it is, of course, impossible to draw up hard and fast rules, for the structure of power varies from territory to territory. Speaking generally, there is a great deal to be said for Dr Herbert Spiro's advice to constitution-makers:

Self-conscious intellectuals without experience in 'the exercise of practical power should ideally be kept out of positions of leadership. But . . . do not exclude any groups aspiring to a share of political power for any longer than may be necessary for reasons such as protection of the constitutional system from totalitarian enemies. . . . Provide units of politics smaller than the whole system itself, either geographical (such as member states or local governments) or functional (such as congregations or unions), in which groups temporarily excluded at the centre of policy-making can assume responsibility for self government.*

The chance, moreover, for white men in Rhodesia or Kenya to shut themselves up in well-defined 'fortresses' is small, except perhaps in Southern Rhodesia, but even there the disparity of numbers between white and black is great. Neither is there a numerous class of poor whites to confuse the issue. A majority of English-speaking Rhodesians think that a policy of all-out *apartheid* would only be possible within the framework of the Union of South Africa; and most of them are sufficiently fearful of Afrikaner rule – and an unaccustomed role as a minority group – to make such a course of action impracticable.

The future seems to lie with economic integration, and further economic development. Existing progress has already brought wider opportunities for Africans. The educated African in Rhodesia may be embittered by colour prejudice; but as long as improvements continue to be made, and as long as he has a well-paying job and hopes of future advancement, it is unlikely that he will rebel. The trouble in the Middle East grew out of the failure of the feudal *élites* to modernize their countries; the rising of the French workers in 1848 similarly was not so much a rebellion against the Industrial Revolution, but was caused by its absence; there were not enough jobs to absorb the growing urban proletariat. The same need not be true in Rhodesia, though the question will have to be faced with particular urgency in the Portuguese territories. Urbanization, better conditions, and hope will continue to maintain public order, as long as governments act firmly and justly.

The multi-racial states south of the Congo may in fact turn out to be much more stable than their critics think. The white national bourgeoisie is well entrenched, their administration relatively strong and efficient, whilst African opposition is

* H. J. Spiro, *Government by Constitution: The Political Systems of Democracy*, New York (Random House), 1959, pp. 210, 296.

divided, both on the territorial and the international plane. Some of the newly-created African states, especially in the French-speaking part of the continent, have in fact experienced more violence and disorder – though with less publicity – than the multi-racial countries; and the position does not seem likely to change in the immediate future.

The question of general economic development is in turn intimately linked to the general problem of how to shift skilled manpower and capital to underdeveloped countries for their greatest mutual advantage. Left-wing propaganda, by dint of steady repetition, has driven home the idea that, though communism may be unpleasant, it does do the job in under-developed societies; it delivers the goods faster than anybody else. This simply is not true of areas of white settlement such as the Belgian Congo, Kenya, or the Federation. Rhodesia, for instance, possessed until recently one of the fastest-growing economies in the world.* The Western powers still have more qualified people and more capital to send abroad than the East; they can do the job not only more humanely but also faster and more efficiently because they are less doctrinaire in their economic approach than a communist country is likely to be.

Both individual migrants and capital, however, need incentives. The only alternative is the use of force. Like the Portuguese attitude to Africa and the British to Australia, the Russians originally regarded distant provinces such as Siberia as a place of exile for political prisoners or criminals. *Degradados* were at one time similarly employed to settle Angola. But now the potential wealth of Siberia and the demands of a much more highly integrated and developed economy have led the Russians to use economic incentives. The old-time explorer or pioneer or political prisoner is now as useless in Siberia as he is in Africa. The old-style Boer farmer, a frontier specialist, has likewise given way to a new kind of specialist – a trained

* The Rhodesian economy for several years was expanding at the rate of 9 per cent per annum. See C. Prendergast, 'Fastest Growing Country in Africa', in *Fortune* LVII (March 1958), p. 122.

expert with capital and skill to practise a more intensive kind of agriculture. The effort to develop secondary industries again has called for a different sort of settler, a man with manual, administrative, or business skill.

No state in Africa, except perhaps South Africa, can provide its own trained people and capital to develop the land; without the necessary infusion of new blood and capital, countries will remain poor for generations, for there is not enough labour or skill available. It was for this reason that the Portuguese, though established in Africa since the sixteenth century, made relatively little impression on native society. There were not enough of them; and foreigners were not usually let in. The Indians and Goanese who were allowed into Moçambique were responsible for much of its economic growth; and the three hundred Boer trekkers who were permitted to settle in Angola similarly helped to pacify and develop that area.

The most striking justification for a policy of intensive immigration is to be found in the history of the United States. Between 1820 and 1930, 65 million emigrants left Europe, and of these 53.8 million went to America.* Earlier still, the enforced migration of slaves had added vast numbers, estimated as high as fifteen million, to the population of North and South America. Although conditions were harsh, the transported African, freed from his tribal life and given opportunities to acquire new skills, advanced and was assimilated more quickly than the native Indian population. Immigration, moreover, provided the United States with a fast-expanding internal market and thus gave a great stimulus to its economic development.

The changing nationality of the immigrants to the United States and preoccupations with supposed dangers to America from 'less assimilable elements' led to a policy of selective immigration, embodied in the quota system after 1921. At

* On emigration statistics and problems see W. S. and E. S. Woytinsky, *World Population and Production: Trends and Outlook*, New York (Twentieth Century Fund), 1953, pp. 70, 71, 77, 104 ff.

first North-west Europe had provided the bulk of newcomers to America, mostly moderately well-off farmers and skilled workers; but after 1880 Southern and Eastern Europe began to send the majority of immigrants; they were generally landless peasants or unskilled workers who filled the labour needs of the new industrial cities.

In Africa it worked the other way. Non-specialists, adventurers and drifters were the first to come to Africa; they acted as prospectors, hunters, casual farmers, and transport-riders. Economic changes, urbanization, and the growth of industries have now forced the change to a specialist emigrant who has skill or knowledge that the colony needs and can pay for. Few unskilled or poor individuals are allowed into multi-racial Africa.

Yet Africa is one of the world's last remaining frontiers – what it needs is neither restrictions nor birth control but immigrants. There is a widespread misconception that Africa south of the Sahara is overpopulated. This view is not in accordance with the facts. Over much of tropical Africa the birth rate averages about 1½ to 2 per cent per annum, which is not an unusual rate of increase. The density of population, furthermore, is extraordinarily low; in Northern Rhodesia, for example, it is 6.3 per square mile. Bantu Africa's major problem is that there simply are not enough hands to do all the jobs needed – be it clearing the land of tsetse fly, building dams, or opening new factories. Under these conditions, there is no relevance in advocating birth control – it is surely not suggested that the empty kraal is the happy kraal; nor is it any more reasonable to limit immigration into Africa or to drive out enterprising immigrants like Indian traders and business men (as may probably be done by African boycotts in Buganda).

The policy of selective immigration, moreover, may possibly have been overdone. Governments often act as if they can pick the right kind of settler; but who can tell who will succeed in a colonial situation, and who can predict what kind of people are needed in a developing economy? Economic planning is a very difficult matter, and a policy of rigid control may

94

well result in keeping out good men without securing the people wanted. A refugee without recognized skill or capital who appears before an immigration selection board today may well be turned down. Yet thousands like him helped to develop America, Israel, and Western Germany, all of which benefited from their non-selective approach. Nowadays, many of the men like Rhodes, or Barney Barnato, who helped to make South Africa, would probably not get into Rhodesia or Kenya.

What is needed is freedom to go where one thinks best, and the individual settler is in a much better position to decide where his advantage lies than even the ablest planning authority. As far as emigration is concerned, the flow of settlers is not like the flow of water out of a tap, something that can be turned off and on by all-wise and all-seeing economists and sociologists, as the occasion seems to warrant. If the tap is shut too often, the flow may well dry up. In the long run, liberality pays, for the man who failed at home or never had an opportunity of displaying his abilities in England or Portugal may well succeed in a new country like Africa. This was certainly true of many who came to America and made good, despite the most discouraging kind of background. Furthermore, to take only immigrants from one nationality may also have the unintended effect of reducing the chance of compromise and accommodation with the indigenous Africans. In Africa, a homogeneous settler area tends to be self-sufficient and often acts as if accommodation were unnecessary, while some national diversity may well act as a general kind of stimulus to intelligent adaptation.*

Neither should public authorities worry too much if a high rate of immigration goes hand in hand with a high rate of emigration. If immigrants should not be kept out, neither should

* Foreign observers have noted a rising sense of colour consciousness in Luanda and Lourenço Marques as Portuguese settlers have increased in number and become self-sufficient white communities. The growing number of semi-skilled and skilled artisans has brought the same kind of racial tension and economic clash as is to be found in Rhodesia.

they be hoarded like gold! Rhodesians, fearful about their high rate of re-emigration, often tend to forget that the United States during the great immigration boom of the nineteenth century had a re-emigration rate of 25 per cent. Re-emigration is not necessarily a bad thing, for it is in everybody's interest that the man who will not or cannot settle down should move to where he can fit in more easily.*

African opposition to increased settlement need not necessarily stand in the way of immigration. It stems sometimes from a feeling of inferiority, and sometimes from a deep-seated fear that the immigrants will never allow them to catch up, or that the presence of a European minority will make the creation of an African state impossible. This resistance is analogous to past movements that arose in the United States against immigrants from Europe. Native-born American Protestants thus organized movements like the 'Know Nothing Party' in the 1850s, or the 'Ku Klux Klan' after the Civil War, to attack Irish, German, or Slavic newcomers. There was nothing enlightened about this resistance of the American workers; it sprang from a fear of change and competition. The new immigrant often did better than the 'old' immigrant and, like the conservative African, native-born Americans resented their success. But Africa, like America in the past, needs to import labour as fast as it can, especially since it is cheaper

---

* Exact figures are not as yet available for the Federation, though they form the topic of a considerable amount of local controversy. J. Isaac, in *Economics of Migration*, London (Trench Trubner & Co.), 1947, p. 63, quotes estimates for other countries. The estimate of United States re-emigration for the period 1821 to 1924 is 30 per cent, and for the Argentine for the years 1857 to 1924 the estimate is 47 per cent. Figures for some African countries are:

> Angola (1958): approximately 60 per cent,
> Kenya (1957): approximately 40 per cent (higher rate than in previous years),
> Tanganyika (1957): approximately 70 per cent,
> Northern Rhodesia (1957): estimate 75 per cent,
> Southern Rhodesia (1957): estimate 25 per cent,
> Nyasaland (1957): estimate 50 per cent,
> Total for Federation (1957): estimate 39 per cent.

for an underdeveloped country to bring in trained men from outside, at no cost to itself, than to train them all on the spot. Paradoxically, it may thus be the countries which encourage immigration which will have least to fear from social and economic problems in the future.

Chapter 3

BLACK NATIONALISM

THE conquest of Africa was but a chapter in a much bigger story. From the Middle Ages onwards, civilized Europe began to push outwards against a multiplicity of tribal frontiers on its Celtic and Slavonic fringes. Knights on horseback, in heavy armour, usually got the better of lightly-armed tribal irregulars. The conquerors were also economically superior. Dutch and German settlers, for instance, who found new homes for themselves in tribal Prussia, wielded heavy iron ploughshares which enabled them to clear dense forest and bush land which the indigenous Prussians could not penetrate with their light 'scratch-ploughs'. Later, when European expansion continued overseas, the same story was repeated in different ways, and, by the end of the last century, the limits of white settlement had been pushed right into Central Africa.

There were many parallels between the old and the new tribal frontiers. European military science again proved irresistible. So did European methods of production. In Southern Rhodesia, for example, white farmers with modern ploughs, and later with tractors, were able to work the heavy red soils that African farmers, using only hoes, had neglected in favour of lighter sandy soils. Only the Europeans could work minerals at great depth, or build railways, telegraph lines, and roads: and tribal society had no effective way of dealing with these problems. The same was true in the field of ideas. The African medicine-men and soothsayers continued a tenacious underground warfare against Christ, but they had no organized theology that could have resisted the white man's religion in open combat. The cultural gap between nineteenth-century capitalism and African tribal society proved, in fact, infinitely vaster than that which had existed between feudalism in its various forms on the one hand, and the different tribal cultures of medieval Europe on the other. The vanquished in Africa, moreover, were of a different colour from their conquerors; the defeated and their children and their children's children were black; the badge of the conquered was the badge of colour. Assimilation therefore proved even more difficult than in medieval Europe, and a new kind of society came into existence in which cultural, social, and racial differences began to correspond with each other to an unusual degree.

The Europeans, for their part, did not constitute a single, homogeneous group any more than the Africans did. They included men of many different nationalities, professions, creeds, and social aspirations. But they did, nearly all of them, stand for a new way of life, the culture of machines and of the cash-nexus. This was true even where the immigrants made their living on the land, for white farmers also employed complex mechanical implements and thought in terms of money-values rather than of mere subsistence. The whites were rarely to be found at the bottom rung of the economic ladder; they were seldom unskilled workers, but were, nearly always, supervisors, skilled artisans, technicians, businessmen, landowners, and industrialists.

African society, on the other hand, became much more sharply differentiated. Village society was profoundly affected by conquest; but the pace of change was extremely uneven, with the result that the Africans became an extraordinarily varied collection of people. At one end of the scale, there were some wealthy contractors and professional men as western in outlook as their white compatriots. At the other end, there were still tribal hunters who would not have been much out of place in the Germany of Tacitus. Between these two extremes were vast groups of Africans who still kept one foot in the tribal community and another in the city. They faced problems of readjustment of extraordinary complexity.

These social and economic contrasts were reflected in the different political ways in which Africans reacted to conquest.

The older kind of leader looked back to the tribal past and dreamed of the days when custom ruled supreme, when land was unlimited, when measures against soil erosion and other new-fangled white devices were unheard of, and when men did not have to worry about sending their children to school. Something of this reaction to modern life was often expressed in independent African churches of the Zionist type, where pagan, Christian, and Jewish beliefs strangely blended, where polygamy was usually sanctioned, and where social protest took on a religious colouring. It is not easy to unravel the complicated strands of animism, Christianity, nationalism, and economic aspiration that went into this new kind of African protest. But one thing is clear – it was not merely colour-discrimination which caused a sense of oppression and insecurity among many backward Africans, it was the disruption of tribal society.

In the John Chilembwe riots that occurred in Nyasaland in 1915, the seeds of a more modern type of African nationalism were certainly present; but perhaps even more important was the reaction of tribal Africans to the impact of Westernization. The protests were often expressed in semi-religious terms that resembled the outbursts of Old Testament prophets against the avarice of great landlords and the dishonesty of employers. The movement of the Prophet Kimbangu in the Belgian Congo and the *Dini Ya Misambwa* along the Kenya-Uganda border bore similar characteristics. The reaction was not uniform. Where the Europeans fully dominated tribal society, or where a strong sense of tribal identity did not exist (as was the case among the Mashona of Southern Rhodesia, who were already a broken people before the whites arrived), this type of response did not occur to the same extent. Sects like *Maya Chaza* in Southern Rhodesia thus condemn some European usages, but are not outwardly anti-European. In regions such as the Belgian Congo and Kenya, however, where there were just enough whites present to disturb tribal life, but not enough to dominate it, anti-European sentiments were much more widely present, and so the *Watu wa Munga* (the People of God) sect that sprang up among the Kikuyu in the 1920s condemned almost everything of European provenance.*

Gradually, preachers and prophets were replaced by movements of a more modern type, whose leaders were drawn, not so much from backward labour migrants, but from the modern, western-orientated intelligentsia, familiar with urban life and its problems. The new men of Africa were not at first revolutionary-minded. In Southern Rhodesia, for instance, the urban associations formed from about 1905 onwards were conservative and accommodating in character; they did not try to challenge the white men's powers but only asked for limited concessions.

When the 'copper revolution' hit Northern Rhodesia in the late twenties and thirties, African welfare societies sprang up along the Northern Rhodesian railway belt, and English-speaking black teachers, hospital orderlies, and clerks banded together in clubs to discuss matters of common interest. In the forties, the scattered African associations which existed in Northern Rhodesia and Nyasaland amalgamated into congresses that aimed at uniting all sections of Africans, and these bodies gradually became more and more radical. The scheme of federating Northern Rhodesia, Nyasaland, and Southern Rhodesia into a new kind of political association was bitterly opposed by many educated Africans as meaning the end of their hopes for black-dominated states north of the Zambezi. Radical congress movements began partly as a result of the movement towards closer union of the three territories.

Nationalism was further stimulated by the Second World War, the break-up of the European empires in Asia, by the example of European political and social movements, the new knowledge or half-knowledge derived from the white daily newspapers, and the influence exerted by Africans who had gone abroad as students or soldiers. There were also economic

* Psychologically, movements like Mau Mau or separatist Churches are a reaction against Western society, and they contain a messianic element that can lead to disastrous violence or to disillusioned apathy.

causes, such as the sharply rising cost of living that accompanied the War and its aftermath.

Shifts in British imperial policy also played an important role. The twenties and thirties were the age of pre-Keynesian economics. The government official was a specialist in law and order rather than an agent of general economic development. The latter was left to the private enterprise of individual entrepreneurs, mostly immigrants from Europe and Asia. Development was concerned with the production of raw materials for world markets, and there was little secondary industry. The *laissez-faire* economics of the time found expression in the doctrine of financial self-sufficiency. Colonies got small imperial subsidies to start them off, but then they were expected to look after themselves; the richer colonies pushed ahead, while the poorer ones could hardly afford the most essential public services. The machinery of administration was simple; one man could effectively supervise the affairs of a whole territory, and Governors were permitted a great deal of freedom. The Colonial Office interfered occasionally to keep things on a straight course, but the last word was usually left to the man on the spot – especially at a time when the British public took little interest in imperial affairs, when colonial issues were debated before an empty House of Commons, and even the negrophiles were concerned with preventing abuses rather than putting forward positive policies.

The constabulary approach was ingrained in most of the administrators. Peace and order had to be maintained, taxes collected, life and property made secure. The main problems of government were administrative in kind, rather than economic or constitutional: and the officials thought in terms of rural rather than urban issues; they were convinced that there was infinite time ahead. Africa would be slowly modernized by the creation of viable economies based on the export of crops and minerals which in time would pay for improved governmental services. In the meantime the main task was that of laying firm administrative foundations, and in the thirties indirect rule became the order of the day. The traditional

102

native authorities, often neglected in the past, received official recognition as the agents of imperialism; their surviving powers of jurisdiction obtained legal sanction; they were given wider financial responsibility and increased status. This policy was thought to combine the best of the old and the new, preserving the main indigenous institutions of government while transforming them into the means of modernizing Africa.

At the end of the thirties and the beginning of the forties, there were sharp changes in the emphasis of British colonial policy. Tropical Africa entered upon the threshold of industrialization. The need for a stabilized urban labour force and for social reforms became more clearly recognized. Colonial government, meanwhile, became a much more complex affair; the District Commissioner who once ruled alone had to collaborate with a steadily growing number of experts, and there was a considerable expansion in administrative staff. The position of the Governor especially changed. The old type of proconsul, like Sir Harry Johnston in Nyasaland, whose régime could fairly be described as 'one of benevolent autocracy tempered only by financial stringency' gradually died out. The typical Governor became more of a moderator rather than a maker of policy, though times of emergency could still bring a reversion to the older pattern.

The changing pattern of government was also influenced by military factors. A nineteenth-century East African Governor, for instance, knew perfectly well that, if the worst came to the worst, there was always a considerable strategic reserve in India to fall back upon. This power reservoir was rarely used, for British rule was profoundly unmilitary in character; nevertheless, the 'big stick' was available in the Indian cupboard, and Indian troops were used as far afield as Abyssinia. The modern Governor, however, is in a very different position. The age of Sikhs and gunboats has largely come to an end, a fact that is not always understood by left-wing or right-wing politicians in Great Britain! The new-style authorities have had to adjust their policy to a multiplicity of interrelated pressures, which are much stronger in character than those with which their predecessor had to cope.

At the same time, there were profound changes of economic policy. Public investment became a recognized aim.* Assistance was no longer to take the form of a continuing subsidy towards the recurrent cost of government, but was to consist of injections at key points of the economy for the purpose of stimulating development; educational aid was itself looked upon as a kind of economic pump-priming. Once an African country had been got to its feet, it would be able to expand its public services and attract more capital from the outside. Until it could 'take off' by its own engine-power, and sustain its future growth from its own savings, the British public would have to subsidize the colony. This economic process was to be accompanied by the building up of independent African states, which would, however, still continue as members of the Commonwealth.

This new interpretation of the imperial trusteeship principle made a considerable impression not only in Africa but also overseas. There was an end to the days when a colonial debate in Parliament would not disturb public apathy, and passions began to be stirred by events on the continent as rarely before. The old belief in infinite time ahead went by the board, to be replaced by a new kind of doctrine which envisaged Africa almost as a kind of express train with a fixed time-table which passengers were supposed to know or else risk missing the train – or even getting crushed on the line!

In Africa itself, leadership of African political movements has now passed to congresses, political parties, and trade unions, led by educated, urbanized Africans, who consider that the final object of imperial trusteeship should be the creation of black national states. These men are often anti-tribal; they want freedom to participate in the modernization of their country; they speak in terms of democracy, parlia-

* See Sir Andrew Cohen, *British Policy in Changing Africa*, London (Routledge & Kegan Paul), 1959, for an excellent account of British policy by a most distinguished public servant.

ments, national self-determination, and universal suffrage; and they dispute with the Europeans for positions of power and privilege – sometimes by violence, sometimes by peaceful means.

In the fight against the 'settler enemy', the differences between the two African groups – the modernizers and the tribalists – may sometimes be obscured, but they do exist. The mass of Africans is still not westernized, and urban leaders can only gain mass support by appealing to the suspicions of the illiterate, as well as to the aspirations of the educated. African nationalism thus presents the countenance of Janus, the ancient Roman god, who was represented by his votaries with one face towards the past and another facing the future; congress leaders must speak with two voices. Sometimes they talk in terms of modern states, ruled on the European liberal principle of one man – one vote, and equipped with all the white man's political and technical know-how. In addition, they also try to cash in on the conservative villagers' distrust of government-sponsored improvement schemes; Africans are warned against measures designed to improve agricultural techniques; there is vicious propaganda against white clinics where black women are supposedly being sterilized; attempts are made to prevent cattle inoculations on the grounds that the government is trying to poison the black man's stock, and simple tribesmen have been led into hopeless trials of strength where the result was a foregone conclusion.*

The two contradictory elements in African nationalism, the rural and messianic on the one hand, and the urban and rationalist on the other, are sometimes resolved by an intensely emotional personality-cult, reminiscent in certain ways of Italian Fascism; the new leader then appears as a Moses destined to lead his people into a Promised Land where social and economic problems are miraculously solved. Fascism, the creed of the disappointed, the economically threatened, and the intellectually marginal men, also provides certain other

* Cf. the Gwembe incident in Northern Rhodesia over the moving of Tonga tribesmen away from an area to be flooded by the Kariba Dam.

parallels, especially the doctrine of the struggle between the 'have' and the 'have-not' nations. This doctrine, which assumes a conflict of interest between the satiated Western countries and the poor but virtuous 'have-not' nations, was originally designed by Fascist thinkers in Italy who thereby tried to lift the notion of a class struggle from the national to the international sphere whilst cementing the unity of their own nation in common opposition to the foreigner. It now forms the stock-in-trade of many African leaders.

But all the same African nationalism is a very real thing. However exaggerated and crude black protests may sometimes be, they do represent the often fumbling efforts of African leaders to improve the condition of their countrymen. African grievances are obvious and genuine; and the nationalism in which they find expression is itself the inevitable product of Western conquest, which provided the essential framework of unified states, improved communications, common languages, widespread literacy, and which was responsible in the first place for breaking down the tribal barriers of old.

African nationalism also stands for something more than merely economic aspirations. For Africans now insist that they be treated with greater respect. They want the parity of esteem which all too often is denied to them, not only by the negrophobe's open abuse but also by the painful conviviality and genteel condescension that sometimes prevail at 'advanced' inter-racial tea-parties. The mystique of *négritude* and the talk of an 'African personality' symbolize the efforts of Africans to restore their inner dignity, even if the means adopted are often exaggerated. To counter the white man's pride of race, many Africans adopt a similar ideology. They are suffering from a 'colonial mentality' and seek to compensate for self-doubt by aggressive assertions of African virtues and imperialist evils.[*]
Confidence and maturity will probably bring more objective

[*] See G. Jahoda, *White Man: a Study of the Attitudes of Africans to Europeans in Ghana before Independence*, London (Oxford University Press), 1961.

and realistic views. Meanwhile, in rejecting the European's contention that pre-conquest Africa was a tribal jungle, where life was 'nasty, brutish, and short', African nationalists romanticize the past and discover hidden virtues in the black folk-soul.

Léopold Senghor, the poet-politician from Senegal, muses over the mystic qualities of blackness, while Kenyatta, the Kikuyu leader, talks about Africans being conditioned to 'a freedom of which Europe has little conception'. Some black intellectuals, especially in French-speaking West Africa, also think that Africans are distinguished by the spiritual depth of their suffering; this ideology sometimes bears a resemblance to the beliefs of many East European historians that the Ruritanian fatherland had acquired special spiritual merit by saving Western Europe from Turks, Tartars, and Asians. *Négritude* is complemented by another supposedly unique quality – *sagesse*, the art of living, a feeling for nature that Europeans, obsessed with rational and technological knowledge, have lost. This ideology is European romanticism all over again in African dress and is similar in character to those products of Teutonic mysticism that extolled the murky depths of Germanic folk-feeling at the expense of the shallow rationalism supposedly typical of Frenchmen and Jews.

The African case, however, does not rest on this kind of reasoning alone, and many African leaders will put forward arguments of a much more convincing kind. The justification of African nationalism is morally the same as that of its Polish, Afrikaans, or Irish equivalent. Racial discrimination and the denial of political and economic privileges will stunt men's growth and interfere with the fullest utilization of human talents. Alien rule itself is a denial of Western values and indefensible in the long run. Africans must not be artificially restricted from access to our civilization; there must be no selective giving. Even a non-racial civilization test can be an offensive thing, for it is highly insulting to a literate African to be told that he or his parents are uncivilized. Africans argue, moreover, that they must have a chance of acquiring the arts

107

of government. Newly independent countries admittedly make mistakes, but only fools resolve never to go into the water till they have learned how to swim.

Furthermore, the denial of economic, as opposed to political, opportunities is not merely morally wrong, it is also inefficient. For a society that arbitrarily denies itself the talents of many of its members is heading for economic suicide. Even if it avoids this fate, growth will obviously be impeded if the positions of power are confined to a few whites. This problem is by no means limited to Africa alone. 'The expansion of Prussia must end', an honest old Junker once said, 'as soon as there are no longer enough Prussian noblemen left to fill all the leading jobs.' The same might be said of a modern industrial economy. If commerce and industry can only recruit their leaders from one section of the community, economic growth sooner or later is bound to slow down. Equality of opportunity is essential, and the acceptance of an African *élite* into the ruling class would, in fact, increase economic efficiency and maintain social stability.*

The more radically minded Africans will go further. Only a black government representing all the black people can mobilize the total resources of the country; only a black ruler can

* In judging the economic colour bar, it should be remembered that administrative practice does not always correspond to legislation. The economic colour bar is being steadily eroded. Inside Salisbury, many Europeans do employ African builders, law or no law! In addition, it is perfectly legal to employ African. *contractors*. New areas outside the Salisbury municipal limits are employing Africans in much larger numbers still. Legislation is, therefore, becoming greatly modified in practice because the state machinery is not strong enough to enforce it against the will of would-be employers. The new Industrial Conciliation Bill in Southern Rhodesia recognizes African trade unions and legislation is being prepared to establish an apprenticeship system for Africans.

Then too there is the practical versus the theoretical impact of the colour bar. Rhodesians think colour laws are made for their convenience. Land Apportionment Act or not, African families, complete with babies, live next to Whites. In any case the colour bar has greatly diminished in intensity; Africans got pushed off the pavement thirty years ago, today they ride the escalator with whites. But the more the colour bar is relaxed, the harder it is to bear.

get the fullest cooperation of his people; only a Touré can dare to call for *travail obligatoire* in the independent Republic of Guinea to make up for lack of capital. Some early experiments apart, both the British Colonial Office and British settler communities have mostly abstained from forcing Africans to work on projects for the common or local good. African nationalists possessed of absolute power could, however, follow the Russian pattern of communal labour by giving the Africans a greater sense of participation, while their leaders would be inspired by a greater sense of urgency for the uplifting of their people. Some African leaders take an even more extreme position and talk in terms of expropriating the whites; they argue that all would be well if the European farms, mines, and factories, with all their profits, were taken over by the black people to whom they should properly belong.

Chapter 4

THE WHITE MAN'S CASE

THE case for African nationalism has made a great impression overseas, and nowhere has the impact been stronger than amongst white intellectuals, who have played a major share in forming our contemporary image of Africa. Less attention has been paid to the point of view of the white settlers, who have, after all, been more concerned with making their living than with arguing their right to do so. No one, however, can think about society without making value judgements, and the settler's case, like that of his opponents, rests in the last instance on certain fundamental assumptions.

Equality, the white man might argue, is an ideal; it is a criterion of justice whereby society periodically judges itself while recognizing that no democratic state has ever managed to attain this ideal in full. Throughout history social groups have organized themselves into hierarchies, for – except on the most primitive level – there has always been a need to provide for a ruling group and a corps of specialists who were given certain privileges in order to hold the people together and raise production. The hierarchical structure of society represented the price which any large group had to pay for its cohesion. The temple priests of ancient Egypt thus received privileges in return for a variety of agricultural, scientific, political, and religious functions which were essential to the country's survival. The grant of special rights to feudal lords during the barbarian invasions of Europe was just as unavoidable; the mounted knight and his strong castle had to be maintained by the labour of serfs, for society depended on the protection given to it by the armoured horseman's mace and lance. Industrial states, be they communist or capitalist, also grant great privileges to all kinds of people – planners, super-

110

visors, technicians, or engineers – no matter what phraseology
is used to defend this practice.

There is nothing wrong with this kind of discrimination,
provided some sort of balance is maintained between privileges and functions, and provided society does its best to look
after its weaker members. The social pyramid will only topple
over when this balance is no longer maintained: when, for
instance, the tough-fisted but hard-working French nobleman
becomes the titled parasite at Versailles spending his time
reading philosophy, coining *bons mots*, and making love.
Society, in other words, needs to determine at what point
group privileges become too expensive a luxury to maintain,
and also how big should be the share that can be made
available to the masses. As far as this share-out is concerned,
modern industrial society is in a better position than any that
have gone before it – the cake is larger than it ever has been
and so everyone can have a bigger slice.

The settler's case thus must ultimately rest on his functions,
and the colonist asserts that the contribution which he has
made and is still making to the future of Africa justifies special
privileges for his group. He asserts that 'his role is a progressive one'. Equality, he argues, should therefore be regarded as a 'regulative principle of justice', not as an absolute
ideal that can be enforced here and now.

African nationalists deny this point of view. They commonly regard equality as an absolute, something that can be
enacted by political means or by a code of law. Their doctrine
is grounded ultimately in the doctrines of seventeenth-century
Christian radicals and those of eighteenth-century thinkers.
The *philosophes*, the intellectuals of their age, taught the
French revolutionary leaders, some of whom then seized on
the principle of equality to attract the poor. The revolutionary
leaders acted as if the principle of equality could be imme-
diately attained. But to get equality, Robespierre argued,
liberty must be suppressed if necessary.

This view bitterly clashed with the principle of liberty
(without social equality) which was taken up by many English

merchants and factory owners during the age of the Industrial Revolution, when they wanted a mobile society, free from outmoded state regulations. But, as the American philosopher Niebuhr points out, the belief in equality was much more dangerous than the faith in liberty. Many social groups benefit from the latter, and a balance of power came into being among the various pressure groups. Some of the advocates of equality, on the other hand, represented an intellectual *élite* possessed of a Utopian creed, and when they gained power they were apt to set up a totalitarian democracy, under which greater crimes were committed than was possible under the slogan of liberty.*

Africa today is undergoing a re-assessment of the privileges and functions held by colonial Powers and settlers alike. This is a necessary process and can be a healthy one. In the past Europeans have largely monopolized political, social, and economic power, but in return for these, they have made and are still making certain essential contributions; these bear re-examination since they are all too easily forgotten in the light of the new anti-colonial orthodoxy.

To recapitulate, the scramble for Africa was not just a story of a gang of white robbers hurling themselves upon a peaceful continent, where the aborigines lived in a kind of undisturbed anthropological museum. The romantic talk of tribal freedom and leisure in pre-conquest Africa has as little basis in fact as the comparable romanticization of clan life in the Scottish highlands. Pre-conquest Africans were of course not a mass of undifferentiated savages, neither were their communities devoid of history. Pre-conquest Africa in fact produced some noteworthy cultural achievements, the importance of which has become obscured, partly because indigenous civilizations, such as those which once centred on Zimbabwe, had completely decayed by the time the Europeans got to Central Africa.

Yet, when all is said and done, tribal society even at its most

* R. Niebuhr, 'Liberty and Equality', in *Yale Review* 47, 1: 1-14, September 1957.

advanced level implied poverty. The ordinary tribesman accordingly had few choices open to him. The sons of a junior wife in Thonga society in Portuguese East Africa, to take just one example, were not free to prosper and gain status or wealth, until the mines and farms of the Rand and Rhodesia gave them an opportunity to work and acquire goods. Previously, by custom all but the children of senior wives had been committed to an inferior status.* The European was not the serpent in a black garden of Eden. African leisure was usually enforced leisure; when there was a drought or when stronger enemies attacked the village and murdered or abducted the able-bodied, stole the cattle or burned the crops, the survivors had little choice but to sit and starve. It is the modern money economy that for the first time has given to the African the choice of real economic alternatives – the foundation for liberty.

The old tribal ways, moreover, were doomed, if only for purely military reasons. Once the 'gunpowder frontier' started moving inland, the existing tribal structures would have undergone far-reaching changes, even if the Europeans had never intervened. There was no real alternative to conquest.

The scramble for Africa was a multi-racial affair. In Ethiopia, for instance, the Amhara (a kind of *Herrenvolk*) participated on their own account in the share-out and managed to secure a substantial slice of alien territory. So did the American Negro settlers in Liberia who brought extensive tribal territories under their control. In East and Central Africa, Arab and mulatto adventurers penetrated deep into the heart of the continent until they were superseded by invaders from Europe. The long-term alternative to imperialism was not some tribal dreamland, but a kind of rudimentary gunpowder feudalism that could only have kept Africa back. The white Powers won; they did so not only because they were militarily stronger, but also because of their superiority in the fields of economics and ideas. They had something to

* M. Harris, 'Labour Migration among the Moçambique Thonga: Cultural and Political Factors', in *Africa*, 29, January 1959, pp. 50–66.

contribute that straightforward military conquerors like the Amhara had not, and thus they deserved to win.

Imperial conquest was in turn widely accompanied by white settlement and it was precisely in those areas where Europeans found permanent homes for themselves that economic development was most thoroughgoing. The mines, the railways, the factories, the tobacco barns, and the hydro-electric schemes that have now come into being in Central and Southern Africa are not things which the white man stole away from the Africans. They were the fruits of an enterprise in which white and black participated, but in which the lead was always taken by the Europeans, who supplied all the plans, the skill, and the capital.* Africa herself had unskilled labour and natural resources. But these alone would have been of no avail. To take a single example, Ethiopia, which possessed both these assets and remained free from alien rule except for the short period of Italian occupation, is still far more backward than Southern Rhodesia with its comparatively numerous settler population.

The reason for this state of affairs is evident. Economic advancement depends on two kinds of capital: social and physical. The former consists of the skill and capacities of a vast number of technicians, administrators, skilled workers, and industrial entrepreneurs. These people are essential, but they are expensive to train on the spot. It is of course still possible to secure quite a number of such persons on short-term contracts without relying on permanent settlement. But in a world where skills are scarce there is not in existence – as some reformers imagine – a vast reserve army of highly-qualified labour, infinitely mobile, ready to go anywhere at any time, at moderate salaries and on short engagements, until they can be replaced by Africans. To put the matter more simply, it is not nearly as easy to get good hydrologists, agricultural engineers, motor mechanics – and also efficient and

* In Nyasaland, to mention just one example out of many, European planters occupy no more than 2½ per cent of the total land, but account for more than half of the country's exports.

honest storekeepers – to settle down in some underdeveloped country, as some people are apt to make out. The immigrant wants not just higher wages, but also a congenial environment and political security; he will not go out, unless he can secure a higher standard of living than he would get at home.

There are only two alternatives to economically motivated emigration. One is emigration for ideological reasons. The other is compulsion. As far as the former is concerned, few will go abroad for purely altruistic reasons; the 'missionary-artisan' has found few successors, and idealistic clergymen dabbling in agriculture or crafts are rarely a substitute for full-time workers. Compulsion of course is another possibility, and this has been employed to some extent by the Communists for the purpose of opening up the underdeveloped areas of the Soviet Union. Nevertheless, even compulsion is not enough and now that the standard of living is rising in Russia, the Soviet rulers too find that more and more economic incentives have to be used to get Dr Ivanovitch, the able engineering specialist, to settle down in Novosibirsk rather than to remain in Moscow, with its fine libraries, theatres, and laboratories.

A democratic society cannot use the big stick at all; it must rely on the carrot alone, and the carrot necessarily consists of higher living standards and improved status for emigrants. As long as African productivity remains low, the existing sharp differences in living standards are therefore unavoidable, even though the gap must eventually narrow. There is another economic rationale for a vigorous white immigration policy in certain African countries. The new Rhodesian, as mentioned earlier, does not merely bring his physical possessions into the country of his adoption. Equally important is the fact that he imports his skill and training as permanent assets for which his homeland has paid, a major social saving.

The settler, in other words, acts as a social yeast in regions in which development has been held back by disease, malnutrition, poverty, and tribalism. The 'web of kinship', however admirable in its original setting, discourages individual

115

ambition and prevents the accumulation of savings. Communal tenure usually inhibits improved techniques of agriculture, for it may be difficult or impossible to experiment, to improve stock, or to add to the fertility of the soil. There is thus little point in arguing, as some critics do, that the Europeans have taken all the best land. This argument is taken to its extreme by African Congress speakers who complain that when the whites first came into Rhodesia in 1890 they stole all the finest farms by the side of the railway lines! For not only do they take little account of pre-conquest land usage, when much of the land now in European possession – for example, the White Highlands in Kenya – was worked little or not at all. They also make no mention of the way in which subsequent land values depended on improvements, on dips and dams and fences, on roads and railways, on markets and trading facilities, all of which have come into existence as the result of white settlement.

Pioneering, moreover, was no picnic. The belief in Africa's wealth has been vastly exaggerated; few El Dorados have been found. Few Kenya farmers, for instance, have been out of debt until recently. The attack on white exploitation of the land only echoes the beliefs of well-meaning but often ignorant idealists about 'poverty in the midst of plenty', for which the realities of Africa afford few grounds. African poverty is real, and the pioneers soon found it out. In the past the truth has often been obscured by scores of publicity pamphlets and novels about life in the colonies, which helped to create the stereotype of the clean-limbed young Englishman of good family who took his upper-middle-class standard of living to the wild veld, 'the land of Goshen'. In more recent times this kind of dream-settler has acquired a twin brother, the 'pass-the-gin-Goddamn-you-I-need-a-woman' planter of anti-colonialist mythology, who supposedly lives in wicked luxury.

The reality is very different. The early farmer in Rhodesia, for example, whether a demobilized British officer, an Afrikaner *trekker*, or a Jewish cattle dealer, had a hard life. He experimented under unknown conditions, he suffered from

116

lack of markets, his stock died of cattle diseases, he faced all kinds of other unforeseen difficulties. These initial setbacks were inevitable, for the whole complex machinery of civilization had to be built up laboriously from rock-bottom, and it was only gradually that living standards and technical proficiency began to rise.

The opponents of white settlement certainly have a case when they speak about the potentialities of African peasant farming, but there are many tasks which the peasant farmer cannot perform; Rhodesian flue-cured tobacco, for instance, requires a skill in organization and an amount of capital that the ordinary peasant does not possess. Peasant farming, moreover is not something that just happens when there are no whites about. Portuguese East Africa and the Zambezi Valley, for instance, have enormous acres of empty land where no Europeans have settled, but no intensive kind of farming has come into being. For the peasant farmer is like any other; he does not merely need land, he also requires social traditions, skills, physical capital, communications, marketing facilities, a social setting conducive to individual effort, the right crop and the right climate – none of which simply develop by keeping out the whites. It is quite possible to argue that – despite some 'feather-bedding' for white producers during the world slump – it is precisely in a country of European settlement such as Southern Rhodesia that the African peasant has been given his best chance; for white settlement has created marketing and training facilities that have benefited white and black alike. The Southern Rhodesian master-farmer scheme for Africans stands out as the kind of thing that can be achieved in a white man's country, and compares very favourably with the state of unimproved indigenous farming that prevails in many other parts of Africa.

Similar considerations apply to the industrial economies which are now coming into existence on the so-called 'Dark Continent', and which have progressed fastest in areas of white colonization. They also had their origin in European enterprise; until recently Europeans have provided all the know-how and most of the capital for the whole of Africa. Even after intensive Africanization programmes over the past decade, Ghana and Nigeria are still desperately, short of trained personnel. In a country such as Rhodesia, with its relatively numerous white population, the position is much more favourable, even though European settlement has also brought sharp social tensions, centring on the economic colour bar. Nevertheless, in areas where Europeans have settled in the largest numbers, Africans have acquired the most industrial skills. The most outstanding example is the Union of South Africa, which counts more skilled African workers in its labour force, and is able to afford a higher average wage for black men, than any other African country.

The question of African skills is not merely affected by the colour bar but also by questions of status. In Ghana or Nigeria there are no white settlers, but all the same those countries have to cope with the problem of prestige-hungry Standard 7 boys who do not wish to do manual or technical work. Too many Africans aim to be clerks, and this is true in Accra, Lusaka, or Nairobi. To sum up, the fact that Africans have not fully shared in the profits of African development is not merely the result of discrimination; the major reason is the African's lack of social capital, not white wealth.

The question of social capital closely affects in turn the question of physical capital. Capital unfortunately is scarce all the world over – it is not merely a matter of greedy investors needlessly withholding money from poor African states. When Dr Rita Hinden of the Fabian Society argues that 'the intense poverty of colonial areas is directly due to lack of capital', she is talking good sense, but she is unrealistic when she writes that the African states 'must be given their railways and roads and harbours and water and power supplies, they must be equipped with schools and hospitals; they must, in short, be endowed altruistically with a complete foundation of public services'. Altruism can do quite a lot, but it cannot supply the whole of Africa with all the capital required.

As far as private investment is concerned, however, not

all the newly created Afro-Asian states have proved themselves to be good risks. The temptation to confiscate alien property is always great for young and shaky régimes; areas of white settlement on the other hand often provide a more stable framework, and this does much to explain their economic success.

European settlement admittedly brings with it social tensions; by Western standards living conditions for the African masses are still often appalling. But by the standards of a country like Ethiopia, Nigeria, or Liberia, the conditions of the African people in Southern Rhodesia are certainly not bad. Slums, malnutrition, and disease are the results of inadequate economic development and not of colour oppression. Neither are the ill effects of black labour migrancy necessarily due to the impact of white settlement or of colour-bar legislation, as is sometimes asserted by progressively-minded critics. Kampala in Uganda, for instance, has no white settlers, no residential segregation, and no *apartheid* laws. But after two generations of town life, the black workers still leave their wives behind in the rural areas; concubinage is rife in the city and family life hardly exists.*

Whenever whites have entered a country in large numbers, African standards have in fact greatly risen. The future problems of development remain vast, but they require above all two things, industrialization and greater agricultural productivity; vast progress is being made in countries of European settlement in both respects. Africans in fact, to use Lenin's phrase, are 'voting with their legs' to enter Southern Rhodesia – and also South Africa – from territories as far afield as Nyasaland and Moçambique where white settlement is sparse.

To argue, as Tom Mboya does,† that Africans would be

* For an interesting study of Kampala, see A. W. Southall and P. C. W. Gutkind, 'Townsmen in the Making: Kampala and its Suburbs', in *East African Studies*, No. 9, 1956.

† *The Atlantic Monthly*, 203, April 1959, pp. 44–6. For similar views see the Northern Rhodesia *Congress News*.

better off without white settlers, and that colonialism only benefits the mother country or her emigrants, simply ignores the facts of life. In Southern Rhodesia, for instance, Africans are beginning to rise in the civil service and business; they enjoy a comparatively efficient system of hospitals and outstanding agricultural improvement programmes; the figure of African savings is going up, and so is the Africans' general standard of living.*

The belief in exploitation rests on a tacit acceptance of the Marxist labour theory of value, which idealizes the unskilled at the expense of the entrepreneur. Admittedly, it was African unskilled labour which alone has made possible all subsequent development; this factor has all too often been overlooked by Europeans in Africa. But progress has been fast; a country like Rhodesia has managed to compress a century and a half of English social history into two generations as far as attitudes towards unskilled labour are concerned.

In the eighteenth century, English labour productivity was low. The English peasant who drifted into the new towns had not yet had time to adjust himself to the discipline of the factory. A considerable labour force was moreover employed in serving the purposes of conspicuous display as footmen, lackeys, and servants in great houses. The employer's outlook was accordingly a moralistic one; the poor were supposedly idle, vicious, and incapable of responding to economic incentives. This early English stage corresponded to the early days of European settlement in Rhodesia, when the colonists used almost the same terms about the tribesmen from the kraal as English employers had adopted towards peasants from the village. In the nineteenth century English labour efficiency and industrial output rose; it was then discovered that the poor were indeed subject to economic incentives; in fact the mistaken

* African-owned motor vehicles in Southern Rhodesia increased from 924 in 1950 to 3,566 in 1957; in 1957 total African savings in Southern Rhodesia banks, postal savings, and building societies amounted to £2,289,366; wages earned by Africans increased from £18.6 million in 1950 to £46 million in 1957.

view was taken that workers would respond to nothing but economic incentives. Rhodesia has now reached the nineteenth-century stage, though she still has to 'make the grade' into the welfare economics of the twentieth century.

In passing through this development, the Rhodesians managed to avoid some of the worst evils of labour management that characterized the early stages of industrialization elsewhere. Early instances in the 1890s apart, there was no conscription of labour, an expedient which overseas opinion fortunately would not tolerate. The indirect pressure of taxation was certainly employed to add to the tribesmen's need of ready cash, but there was no direct force. The system of early labour migration moreover meant that Rhodesia was spared the evils of women's and children's labour in mines and factories that formed such a characteristic feature of early industrialization in Europe. The tribesmen were thus to some extent cushioned against the effects of early industrialization, though they did not for the time being reap the full benefits of it either.

It seems likely that in areas where Europeans have settled in Africa the territories concerned got their original accumulation of capital at bargain rates, at the price of certain economic, social, and political privileges for the European minority; these special rights weighed less harshly on the masses than the sacrifices demanded by the deliberate under-consumption of a Communist state or the forced labour programme of Sékou Touré in the Republic of Guinea, not to speak of China.

This fact is reflected, interestingly enough, in the size and structure of the military and police forces of the settler countries, a factor that political scientists and sociologists have consistently neglected in the past. For it is one of the most essential features of the Federation that it is profoundly unmilitaristic in character. The average modern state nowadays maintains or aims at maintaining a peacetime strength of between one and two per cent of its population in the fighting forces and the police. In Communist countries the percentage is higher still. But in the various territories of the Federation of Rhodesia and Nyasaland the military and police strength varies between one and two per thousand of the total number of inhabitants. In economic terms this means that a relatively large proportion of the country's national wealth can be used for productive purposes. In terms of political power, the ruling strata are compelled to rely to a much larger extent on peaceful persuasion than is commonly assumed by anti-colonialists. The European population is not militarized in Rhodesia any more than it is in the Union of South Africa. The army's direct political role is insignificant, a factor that sharply differentiates these countries from many of the newly independent states of Asia and Africa.

What of the years to come? There is the major problem of the future realignment of political power. This is usually interpreted by outside critics of multi-racial countries in what might be called the Anglo-centric fashion. Liberals generally imagine that these regions can pass through a development similar to that of Great Britain in the nineteenth century, which successfully enfranchised first of all its middle classes, then its urban, and finally its rural working classes. The fact that the multi-racial countries are also troubled by profound cleavages of race, colour, and cultural tradition, which are largely coextensive with those of social class, is discounted. The liberals argue that the propertied classes will have to make some sacrifices, but criticize settler prophecies of great social disasters as just so much bunkum. The settlers should take the leap into the political dark and they will fall on their feet.

The British parallel is not a good one. Outside Ireland, which never fitted the British pattern and ultimately wrecked the Union, there were no serious minority problems in Britain, since national and class divisions never widely coincided. In nineteenth-century Britain there was much poverty, but nevertheless the country as a whole was rich. It possessed a vigorous and long-established bourgeoisie, and once the country's vast industrial investments had reached the producing stage there was enough for shares all round without a violent overthrow of the social system. At the same time Britain was developing one of the most productive agricultural systems known to history without meeting any serious opposition from the rural proletariat. From about the middle of the century onwards, the British upper strata felt themselves safe from revolution, and they could afford to make many concessions.

As far as the outside world was concerned, Britain was protected by an invincible navy. The ordinary citizen might never see the great ironclads that defended his country and represented British industrial and technical supremacy on the high seas, but he rightly believed that Britain was safe from attack. John Bright and the Webbs were as much children of the age of the two- and three-Power standard as were Newbolt and Kipling. It was indeed this unconscious acceptance of British naval supremacy which contributed so much to the ingrained optimism of British progressives and which made them so indifferent towards questions of military strategy. Liberals in Central and Southern Africa have taken over this general framework of ideas, but they often fail to realize that the experiences of a racially and culturally homogeneous country in Western Europe are of very little significance to a multi-racial African state.

Neither is there any real parallel between a country like Rhodesia or Kenya and areas such as Brazil, the West Indies, or the Southern States of America, though this comparison has sometimes been made by outside observers. In all these former transatlantic plantation colonies, the full assimilation of all the Negro immigrants ultimately became practicable policy. The slaves who were so cruelly transplanted beyond the ocean paid the full price of subsequent liberal policies of absorption; their tribal traditions, languages, as well as their social cohesion, were largely or entirely shattered; the black immigrants became English- or Portuguese-speaking and they ceased to be the nucleus of new potential national groups. The American Negro of today may look a little different from his white compatriot; he may be a little poorer, but he is an American and nothing else, for the American language and the American way of life are the only ones he knows, and in this respect he is exactly like the descendant of a German or

Polish immigrant who has lost his parents' culture and become an American.

In Africa the position is very different. The linguistic and cultural cohesion of the Bantu-speaking peoples was never smashed. They were never Anglicized or Afrikanerized; for numbers alone made such a policy impossible for the white conqueror. Africa resembles much more the minority-ridden lands of the Near East and of Eastern Europe, where the general level of economic development was usually much lower than in Western Europe, and where class, race, and national divisions often tended to coincide, putting added strain on the social structure in times of rapid economic and political change. Nineteenth-century Transylvania, for instance, was in some ways like East Africa today. The landowner was a Hungarian, the peasant a Rumanian, the burgher perhaps a German, the trader a Jew. A man's language denoted his social class and occupation. This position was liable to lead to severe tensions when social struggles began to be overlaid by linguistic conflicts.

The age of nationalism in these regions in fact inaugurated periods of savage collisions. The seeds of strife were laid when the peasant began to go to school, and when peasant-bred intellectuals became their leaders. The peasant's son with a university diploma soon found that his best way of getting on in life was by getting into the civil service, for he had been trained neither for commerce nor industry. In order to get advancement in the bureaucracy, he discovered that he needed political power. His social and economic demands encouraged nationalism, and nationalism in turn set up new tensions. Once political control had been secured, the middle class nationalist insisted on economic control, and often began to attack the alien minorities that did not belong to the charmed circle of the new 'people of the state'.

The new demands tended to follow a certain pattern. There was the cry for land reform, irrespective of its economic consequences, but directed against an alien, property-owning minority. (This stage has now been reached in Kenya.) There

followed the cry for 'adequate' representation of the new
ruling group in the public services, business, and the professions at the expense of the older groups; national considerations everywhere began to outweigh those of efficiency, and
there developed a complex science of how to squeeze aliens by
means of state corporations, by artificially reducing their
numbers in various economic and academic fields, by con-
sumers' boycotts and other means of persecution.

National-social transformations of the type mentioned
above sometimes even led to the physical extinction of the
minorities concerned. Such was the experience of the Anatolian
Greeks and the Ottoman Armenians. The German Jews had a
similar fate, when conditions after the world crisis in the
slump-ridden Fatherland temporarily began to resemble those
of an underdeveloped country. There was nothing the minorities could do in those circumstances but to emigrate; even
the most thoroughgoing attempts at identifying themselves
with their host-nations – as with Jews who intermarried and
adopted German culture – were of little avail. The 'German
citizen of Israelite faith', with his passionate German nationalism and his officer's commission, was never fully accepted as
a German, and was liquidated in the end. Yet he was much
more assimilated to the land of his birth than any European
liberal in East or Central Africa who believes that he can safeguard his future by identifying himself with the forces of
Bantu nationalism.

It might be added that the persecution of minorities did not
necessarily end under Marxist régimes either, even though
class, not race, now became the officially sanctioned criterion
of liquidation. The number of minorities expelled from Communist countries has been immense. They have included the
Germans of East Prussia and Bohemia, the Japanese of Northern Sakhalin, the Magyars of Slovakia, the Bulgarians of
Turkish origin, and a host of others. This point should be of
some interest to white Communists both in North and in
South Africa.

Under the conditions obtaining in poor Near Eastern or

White Settlers in Tropical Africa

Balkan countries the prospects for Western-style parliamentary democracy were extremely dim. This form of government has in fact never flourished anywhere in Eastern Europe outside Czechoslovakia, despite numerous attempts to implant it in uncongenial soil; neither did democracy survive in any Middle Eastern country outside Israel. Its prospects are equally unfavourable in the newly liberated 'Bandung' countries of South-east Asia, where state planning, the prevailing authoritarian traditions, and the fact that the indigenous middle class consists mainly of civil servants, all make the setting up of stable parliamentary régimes very unlikely.*

The position is no different in the new states of Africa, though white liberals, acting under a strange kind of compulsion-neurosis, still insist on prescribing the old parliamentary medicine for all these emergent states. As things are, the new states of Africa cannot and will not be Western democracies, though they may continue to adopt the phraseology of their erstwhile imperial tutors. Power is likely to become highly centralized, or anarchy will probably ensue. To speak defensively of 'guided democracy', 'tropical democracy', or 'African democracy' in this connexion merely means twisting words out of their accustomed meaning. In fact, the only countries where European parliamentary traditions, with their established machinery for peacefully changing the government in power, are likely to survive are those regions where European settlers form a numerous group, and where their political influence remains strong. Some newly-independent African states are likely to become army-ruled countries, like the Sudan. The army, in underdeveloped countries, is sometimes the most Westernized group. Army discipline cuts across local and clan ties; in addition, of course, the army is armed. In the words of a Sudanese apologist:

It is sometimes more democratic to give the people what is good for them instead of what they ask for, specially if they are – as in the

* See article by F. G. Carnell in *The Development of the Middle Class in Tropical and Sub-Tropical Countries*, Brussels (International Institute of Differing Civilizations), 1956.

case of most African States – only 2% to 5% literate and thus sus-
ceptible to all forms of propaganda and too poor to resist a bribe. . . .
We in the Sudan have licked the type of democracy you are mourn-
ing. Before they left the British gave us (read 'imposed on us') a two-
House system, but it was killed in embryo. The wandering and corrupt M.P. was a feature of our Parliament. . . . We got fed up. The
Army came to our rescue. . . .*

The position has unfortunately been obscured by the prevalent habit of measuring European settler countries in Africa
against the standards of Western Europe, instead of those of
other African countries like Egypt, the Sudan, Ghana, or
Guinea. It is this Anglo-centric cast of mind which has led so
able a student of politics as Mr Colin Leys into such a dangerous trap.† He comes to the conclusion that Southern Rhodesia
constitutes in reality nothing but a one-party state, because
the Africans are mostly excluded from power and because the
country is ruled by a small settler-oligarchy. The remedy
accordingly recommended is a very wide franchise.

But Mr Leys, with his English orientation, makes no
attempt to compare the position in Southern Rhodesia with
that in other underdeveloped countries. Had he done so, he
would probably have arrived at very different conclusions. For
it could be argued that it has been precisely the fact that power
has largely been retained in the hands of a relatively limited
group, consisting mainly of Europeans, that has made it
possible for a genuine parliamentary régime to survive. Otherwise Southern Rhodesia would probably have followed the
ordinary Balkan, Near-Eastern, and West African pattern
where authoritarianism – based on a mass-party or a highly-
disciplined army – and anarchy form contrasting and complementary poles of politics.

Few men of left-wing convictions may agree with our
analysis. But an examination of the problems affecting the

---

* Letter from Omer El Zein to *The Times*, quoted in *East Africa and
Rhodesia*, 20 August 1959, p. 1438.
† C. Leys, *European Politics in Southern Rhodesia*, Oxford (Clarendon
Press), 1959.

existing African states does little to bear out the liberal's prevailing mood of optimism with regard to a democratic future for the new Africa. Democracy of the Western type is an almost impossible ideal for backward agrarian societies. Liberty and stability will not easily be secured if Africans seize power, especially where white minorities are involved. The temptation to make the Europeans the universal scapegoats for the tensions and frustrations of primitive society in the throes of rapid transformation is too great. Nkrumah and Bourguiba still use colonialism as an excuse for all their countries' weaknesses. Equally great is the temptation to escape from internal difficulties by foreign adventures, as Nasser has done. Pan-Africanism (like Pan-Germanism or Pan-Slavism) might in fact become just the kind of goal that could divert African peoples from solid development on a limited front to chasing phantoms on a continental scale.

The situation is further aggravated by the fact that African states also suffer from divisions along tribal or religious lines. These conflicts are often hidden from the outsider by reason of the fact that they are expressed in modern political slogans and phraseology; but they exist. The manifold tensions that affect the new states may lead them into anarchy on the old South American pattern. The only alternative to anarchy is likely to be a highly authoritarian kind of government. The exact composition of this may vary. There may be the rule of an educated *élite* wielding a strong party organization, as in Ghana, or a military dictatorship as in Egypt and the Sudan, or a temporary union between the educated and feudal ruling groups as in Nigeria. But power will have to be centralized.

The new states will also have to contend with difficulties arising from the international situation. The new scramble for Africa is on. It is being fought by the weapons of dollar and rouble loans, by means of high-powered propaganda, the armed infiltration of irregulars, and the ultimate diplomatic and military pressures of heavily-armed continental blocs. In these circumstances the outlook for the new states is not a cheerful one. In the last century British liberals rightly used

The White Man's Case

to back small nations struggling to be free. Gladstone's policy of supporting the Christian Balkan nationalities against their Ottoman overlords made some sense, not merely from the religious and economic, but also from the military point of view. At that time the main weight of warfare fell on the infantry; and by and large, a Bulgarian division in the 1870s was about as good as a Russian or an Austrian division; the new Balkan states, therefore, had some chance of defending themselves. After the First World War the industrialization of warfare made the peasant armies largely obsolete, and by 1940 a Balkan division was no longer the equivalent of a German one. The latest developments of military science have changed the military situation further still; only large continental blocs can now wage wars successfully. From the military point of view the new 'Bandung' states are already as obsolete as the air-squadrons with which they now hurriedly equip themselves.

Neither is there any force in the much-repeated arguments that the metropolitan countries should plan their policies so as to win the sympathy of the uncommitted nations of Asia and Africa, which are supposed to hold the future world balance of power in their hands. This point of view neglects the military realities of power and looks upon the present struggle for world supremacy as a sort of ideological beauty competition in which the panel of judges is made up of Asians and Africans! This point of view has little basis in fact; a tough policy against its own settlers will not really add to the strength of the West. Nations are influenced by ideas, but ideological considerations only rarely outweigh economic and strategic factors as the guiding principles of a country's foreign policy. In this respect Asians and Africans are no different from anyone else, and will not be guided by gestures. Not even the wholesale expulsion of all whites from a country like Rhodesia would induce any African state to support NATO, unless the ruling groups of that state felt that its interests were better served by joining the West than by remaining neutral.

It is, accordingly, very doubtful how far the West would be

129

justified in subordinating its interests to the real or imagined demands of neutralists. For, when all is said and done, it is only the strength of the West, and nothing but its strength, which has up to now made it possible for the Afro-Asian countries to afford the luxury of neutralism. Once the West weakens the fate of the new countries is not likely to be any different from that of, say, the Georgian Social Democrats, or the Hungarian National Communists, who were overthrown by the Soviet armies after the First and Second World Wars respectively. To look at the question the other way round, the friendship of all the uncommitted nations would not help the West in the slightest if the West ever allowed its economic and military defences to crumble. The disintegration of Western power would, however, only be speeded up by the contraction of Western influence in areas inhabited by white minorities in Africa; to encourage this process can thus hardly be described as being advantageous to Europe.

Some liberals have taken a different line and have argued that the Europeans in Central Africa should meet the demands of the more extreme African nationalists now, while they still have a chance of doing so peacefully. If they don't, pressure will simply keep mounting and the final bang become all the louder. The mechanics of a revolution, however, are not those of a defective pressure-cooker! Revolutions, like ordinary warfare, require careful planning and well-trained cadres. Before the first shot is ever fired, the key positions in the economic, military, and administrative structure should have been well infiltrated. The state should have become fatally weakened either from the impact of foreign war or from internal decay. More important still, a revolution will succeed best if the ruling class has become a group of functionless parasites and if their régime represents an intolerable drag on the country's future economic development.

As far as the Union of South Africa or the Federation of Rhodesia and Nyasaland is concerned, none of these conditions exists. Their economies are still sound, despite a recent serious recession, their armed forces and administration are

130

reasonably efficient, the key positions are firmly in 'loyalist' hands, and the ruling group represents economic progress. A major political feature of these regions is the fact that the economic leaders, the businessmen, the industrialists, the technicians, the managers, the most advanced farmers, and a considerable section of the skilled workers are Europeans; it is the whites who constitute the new national bourgeoisie without whose cooperation there can be neither economic progress nor an effective revolution; settler nationalism forms the exact equivalent of that middle-class nationalism which has led to the creation of other national states in other, formerly dependent parts of the colonial world.*

The opposition on the other hand is far from united. The African community is itself becoming divided on class lines, which sometimes cut across but at times also correspond to tribal divisions; it would be a serious mistake to suppose that a wealthy African bus-owner in Southern Rhodesia or a successful fish-trader on Lake Bangweolo is now particularly anxious to mount the barricades. The African working class is similarly split, partly because the spread in wages that formerly separated whites from blacks is now appearing within the African working class itself. The rural population also lacks cohesion, due to the fact that one section looks forward into the future, to a régime of individual land ownership, while another section still dreams of the glorious tribal days of old.

From the rulers' point of view, the position is least stable in Nyasaland, the 'Federation's Ireland'. The little country is threatened, not only by a serious land problem, but also by the perils that arise from underdevelopment. Few Europeans have settled in the country; no mines have been developed and almost no factories built, with the result that there is not enough employment in the country for the young. All the

---

* The shift in power from the overseas to the local level has become noticeable not only in the political but also in the economic sphere. For the years 1954 to 1959 the gross investment in the Federation of Rhodesia and Nyasaland amounted to more than £805 million. Of this nearly £581 million was derived from domestic saving and less than £225 million from net borrowing abroad.

same, the likelihood even in Nyasaland of an armed over-throw of power, as distinct from rioting, is remote. Disorders by themselves are not likely to change the balance of power decisively, provided they are handled firmly. If this is done, the possibility of a forcible transfer of power cannot at this point be admitted into the realm of practical politics.

This analysis should of course not be regarded as a plea for doing nothing. The social equilibrium of multi-racial societies might be compared with that of a bicycle – its balance can be maintained, but only provided the rider is going forward rather than trying to stand still or pedal backwards! As far as Rhodesia and Nyasaland are concerned, the future centres on the question of industrialization. The black peoples of the Federation are doubling their numbers every twenty-five years, and unless new industries come into being to absorb the grow-ing urban population, disaster is bound to ensue. The indus-trial revolution will at the same time have to be balanced by an agricultural revolution in the villages, so that they can both feed the towns and give the country-folk a better livelihood.

Economic reconstruction in turn requires some kind of *modus vivendi* between white and black. The South African solution of trying to create separate white and black areas on the principle of *apartheid* has been advocated by some in Southern Rhodesia. But the whites' lack of numbers, their economic difficulties, and the absence of that passionate na-tionalism which forms such a striking feature of Union politics now make its acceptance impossible.

As for the future of the Federation, time will tell. The pre-vailing feeling of political uncertainty has had a serious effect on economic enterprise, especially in the Northern territories, where black governments appear more imminent, and where many entrepreneurs have been unwilling to invest funds, fear-ing that African rule might lead to disintegration. The Feder-ation's constitutional future is still in the balance. Its prob-lems were investigated in 1960 by a Commission headed by Lord Monckton which reported that Federation had brought great economic benefits, but that most politically conscious

Africans still remained hostile. The Commissioners recommended that Federation be continued, but that more powers be handed back to the territories. They also recommended that Northern Rhodesia and Nyasaland be granted a constitutional right of secession. Their proposals, however, met with strong opposition from the Federal Government, which was able to exercise a decisive influence through its constitutional powers and its control over the Federal army and air force.

In 1961 a referendum was held in Southern Rhodesia to determine whether the country should adopt a more liberal form of government. It resulted in acceptance of the new constitution, which gives Africans for the first time representation in the Southern Rhodesian Legislative Assembly. Fifteen members will be elected on a lower roll, which has lower financial and educational qualifications, and the remaining fifty will be elected on an upper roll with higher qualifications; both rolls will remain non-racial in character. The constitution also gives what amounts to full internal autonomy. The United Kingdom is no longer able to interfere with locally made laws, its powers of veto having been replaced by various safeguards which will be exercised on the spot, rather than from London.

The new constitution was opposed on the European side by a right-wing group which contained many of the less prosperous artisans and employees, and the smaller farmers. Some of these people looked towards South Africa for a solution of Southern Rhodesia's problems, but a considerably larger number thought that the country should secede from the Federation and continue traditional policies. The opponents of the constitution also included the National Democratic Party, the major African opposition, which objected to the proposals for very different reasons, arguing that the terms did not go far enough towards meeting African wishes.

On the other side, the United Federal Party, which controls both the Federal and the Southern Rhodesian Assemblies, threw all its influence behind the constitution. It based its campaign on the continued extension of partnership between the races, and argued that the emergent middle class of

African storekeepers, bus owners, contractors, and 'master farmers' should be 'built into' the existing political structure, and that education and property should remain the criteria for political control, even if such a policy should result in an African majority in the more distant future. Fundamentally the party's policy was based on the assumption that political power should form the 'superstructure' of economic power, a view strongly held by most Rhodesian entrepreneurs, whose beliefs in this respect ran oddly parallel to those of their Marxist critics.

For a time the position of the UFP seemed difficult, partly as the result of bitter dissensions with the Imperial Government over constitutional progress in the Northern territories, partly because of a sharp economic recession which had begun to affect the country from about 1958 onwards, and partly as the result of the grave shock to white opinion during the Congo breakdown. In addition, the party faced a small white opposition on its left, recruited mainly from the liberal professions, the Churches, and some of the upper strata in the mining industry, who regarded black rule as inevitable, and hoped to make the transition to it short and painless. The liberals, however, were divided. Some voted against the constitution, but the majority supported it, probably on the grounds that some change was better than none, and in the end the Southern Rhodesian Government attained an overwhelming victory.

Political conflicts have also taken place within the Northern territories of the Federation. The situation there is complicated by the fact that these have remained imperial protectorates, unlike Southern Rhodesia, which since 1923 has had the status of a self-governing colony. The Conservative Government in the United Kingdom, by now well to the left of its predecessors in colonial matters, produced in 1961 a new constitution for Northern Rhodesia. This is based on a complicated system of three voters' rolls, whereby fifteen seats are to be elected from a (mainly white) upper roll, and fifteen seats from an African lower roll, while fifteen seats are to be elected on a national basis. Under pressure from the United Federal Party, which forms the main opposition in the Northern Rhodesian Legislative Council, the government slightly modified the constitution after lengthy negotiations.

Nyasaland, an African territory forced by the United Kingdom into the Federation against the will of white Rhodesian politicians, as well as of African nationalists, has acquired an African-dominated Legislative Council. Nyasaland's political situation was complicated by African nationalist intimidation in the form of arson, physical violence, and attempted murders; but Dr Hastings Banda's Malawi Party won control of the legislature in the elections of August 1961, and promised to take Nyasaland out of the Federation.

While the Federation as a whole continues mainly under European control, Tanganyika, which has a small white population, is progressing towards complete independence under the one-party rule of the Tanganyika African National Union. The country is still economically backward, despite recent injections of British capital, but at least it has achieved political stability. On 1 May 1961, Julius Nyerere became Prime Minister, having already secured a promise of full independence by December. Not even Nigeria achieved self-government in so friction-free a manner. Nyerere's brand of moderate nationalism might show that a multi-racial society in Africa could attain political harmony. He believes that he can succeed

by peaceful political campaigning without intimidation, by a short period of cooperation and partnership in Government before assuming full powers. It is incredible, in the face of the facts of Tanganyika today, that so many other East African nationalist leaders still follow the path of . . . machination and political 'one-up-manship', in preference to vigorous and successful leadership. Tanganyika is a poor country economically. Politically it can be one of the richest in Africa.*

But the problem is much more difficult in Kenya; the Europeans are more numerous and have in the past been hesitant to give up political power. Also the Africans have been bitterly

* *Kenya Weekly News*, 7 April 1961.

divided; there has been some violence and revival of oath-taking ceremonies. A new constitution, promulgated by the Conservative Government in 1960, effectively deprived white Kenyans of their formerly extensive political influence, and the country has now become part of Black Africa. Many Europeans have removed their capital from the country, and some are thinking of making a new start elsewhere. Some thirty-five per cent of the White Highlands has been offered for sale. The Imperial Government, which was responsible for white settlement in the first place, has refused to compensate farmers who wish to emigrate, and has not up to now shown any willingness to safeguard European land titles.

This policy, whether politically justifiable or not, has produced a major economic crisis, for in the twelve months following the Lancaster House constitutional discussions the market value of Kenya Government and East African High Commission stock dropped 18·1 per cent, while industrial shares plummeted 32·5 per cent, reflecting a serious loss of faith in the stability and economic potential of Kenya. Worse yet, almost no new investment has been made. The British Government has agreed to loans and grants of £14·5 million for 1961–2, but this is no long-term solution.

The local Europeans point out that their own small community, the most highly taxed in Kenya, paid about half the country's annual revenue. They also provided about three-quarters of the agricultural produce, including an export surplus of about £20,000,000, and paid out wages of about £10,000,000 p.a. Their farming constitutes the country's economic bed-rock; it is not at all like the absentee landlordism which ruined Bourbon feudalism, or the old Anglo-Irish 'Establishment'. Nevertheless, the settlers fear that their properties will become subject to penal taxation or outright confiscation in the name of land reform. Their fears are being heightened by the statements of African politicians, and by the way white farms, houses, and women are being offered as lottery prizes by unscrupulous Africans who promise the world to their unlettered countrymen, once *uhuru* (freedom) has been attained.*

The White Highlands are now open to purchasers of all races, but there are few buyers because most Africans lack capital as well as experience. The whites argue that if their large, well-run, and highly capitalized farms are taken over by an African government acting under popular pressure, the present economic farming units would be split into African small holdings which would only sustain low-level subsistence farming. As a result exports would sharply diminish, and a considerable proportion of the black labour force would find itself without jobs. This would mean that the land might in fact support fewer people than at present, and the country's cash economy might break down.

The exodus or expulsion of the white farmers would not of course have such serious consequences if the West were in a position to replace these people by a great army of experts willing to live in the bush. This great reserve does not, however, exist; and anti-colonialist thinkers must therefore find some kind of an answer to the problems posed by white emigration from the countries Western anti-colonialists have helped to liberate. Even expert observers have not always recognized the fact that it is often the wealthiest, most skilled and adaptable members of a threatened minority who can most easily make a new start abroad if they are not content with the existing government.

The problem of re-establishing white confidence, therefore, is just as important as the problem of conciliating Africans, unless the whites are to be driven into resistance where they are strong, or into emigration where they are weak. White farmers, entrepreneurs, and technicians are essential to poverty-stricken areas lacking skilled manpower and capital; a white exodus would probably be as serious in its econo-mic consequences as the departure of the Jews from fifteenth-

* For an account of this kind of political demagoguery see the American Negro journalist, Louis Lomax, *The Reluctant African*, New York (Harper and Brothers), 1960.

century Spain or the expulsion of the Huguenots from seventeenth-century France. It remains the task of statesmanship to ease the apprehension of many Europeans who live in the territories under discussion.

The Congo remains split into rival factions. As yet the wealthy Katanga and Southern Kasai Provinces have shown little willingness to pool their resources with the more backward regions. A strong unitary state is obviously preferable to a loose confederation; it would allow a modernizing *élite* to develop the Congo and avoid stagnation and tribal warfare; but at the 1961 conferences at Tananarive and Coquilhatville it appears that only a confederation of states could be agreed upon.

Efforts to reunite the Congo met with more success in July 1961, at the first meeting of the Congolese Parliament for ten months. Cyrille Adoula, the former Minister of Interior and Defence in Kasavubu's government, was chosen as Prime Minister. Adoula, who calls himself a positive neutralist, has shown tact and organizational ability. He appears determined to restore the unity of the Congo, but whether he can fashion an effective government out of these sharply divided groups remains to be seen.

Meanwhile the Congolese economy is deteriorating. Continued political instability and the separation of the provinces of Orientale, Kasai, Kivu, and Katanga hinder efforts at recovery. Exports have dropped, exchange reserves are dwindling, and inflation threatens. Worse, the instability and chaos of the Congo have spilled over into Angola and threaten to produce anarchy there as well.

In 1961 violence broke out in Angola as African nationalists spread terror in tribal villages and European plantations. Although raids on police barracks in Luanda were put down, the north erupted soon afterwards, and revolutionary groups raided over 200 square miles of territory. Driven by fear and a desire for revenge, Europeans formed committees of vigilantes and indiscriminately shot Africans, especially those associated with Protestant missions.

The White Man's Case

The Portuguese forces remained small, in spite of the extra 15,000 troops who were rushed to Angola. The UN Security Council in June 1961 appointed a commission to investigate the war. Bitter guerrilla warfare continued; mutilations, executions, and the burning of villages were the tactics of both sides. By August, thousands of Africans and an estimated 1,000 whites had been killed, and tens of thousands of Africans had fled to the Congo. The Portuguese have gained a number of successes but political reforms are essential; a long Indonesian type of war will be difficult for Portugal to sustain, for it is a poor country and has almost no armaments industry. Furthermore, Angola will prove a hard country to pacify: the Portuguese troops lack mobility, the terrain is difficult, there are few roads, bridges, or airstrips, and dense forests and high grass aid the nationalists.

The Angolan revolt has serious implications for all the surrounding territories. Portuguese Africa's migrant labour is important to the economies of the Federation of Rhodesia and Nyasaland and the Union of South Africa. Railroads carrying goods in and minerals out of Central Africa pass through Angola and Moçambique. The political balance of power will dramatically shift in Southern Africa if Portugal loses Angola.

Information is scarce and not always reliable but it appears that the Angolan revolutionaries are made up of three elements: members of the Force Publique who fled after the Congo mutiny of July 1960, Angolan nationalists, and a small group of Angolan Communists who have been busy forming a revolutionary army since 1959. The two largest nationalist groups are the Angolan People's Union (UPA) under Holden Roberto, based in Leopoldville, and the Movement for the Liberation of Angola, directed by Mario de Andrade, with headquarters in Conakry and Brazzaville. Roberto is pro-Western and has been careful to avoid being linked with Communist front organizations. Andrade, a Lisbon-educated mulatto and former Sorbonne professor, is a Communist.

This is not a spontaneous rising of African nationalists. The struggle has been well planned and organized, and some rebels

139

have modern weapons and show a familiarity with modern guerrilla and terrorist tactics. What is happening in Angola may, in part, be a Communist-inspired war of national liberation.*

The rules for wars of national liberation were laid down by Mao Tse-tung and Liu Shao-chi: first a Communist party is created in the territory, then an underground and united front organization are set up, after which guerrillas can be trained to fight from rural bases and prepare the way for national liberation armies. This sequence has been followed in Angola. The groundwork was laid in 1955 when the Communist Party of Angola was formed and an underground organized. Later, the Communists joined with other groups to form the Movement for the Liberation of Angola (MPLA), led by Andrade. Not until 1959 was the popular front set up – the African Revolutionary Front of Struggle for National Independence of Portuguese Colonies. A series of incidents caused the police to crack down, the Front was established in Conakry, and the training for the war of national liberation began.†

The UPA of Holden Roberto apparently spearheaded the invasion of Angola but soon the African Revolutionary Front was also fighting in the territory. Actual Communist strength in the popular front appears quite small, though Peking was asked for aid, and the leaders went to China in May. Most members probably are sincere nationalists with legitimate grievances.

Nothing is to be gained by ejecting the Portuguese from Africa at the present time. Who is to take their place? None of

* Western critics have scoffed at Portugal's claims of Communist influence but Communist journals and newspapers like *Tass, New Times,* and *International Affairs* have openly claimed credit for the rising; for example see *Kommunist,* February 1961, pp. 88–93. The theory of national liberation movements and their activities in Angola are carefully presented in an article 'Proxies for Communism,' in a liberal American journal, *The Reporter,* 8 June 1961.

† See 'Portugal's Colonial Possessions', *International Affairs,* Moscow, March 1961, pp. 116ff; also Mario de Andrade, 'Freedom will come to Angola', in *Pravda,* 6 February 1961.

the African organizations has as yet established a clear right to rule, nor have they the trained personnel to do so. A power vacuum should be avoided. Peace must first be restored, then a reasonable plan of preparation for independence worked out. The U N can aid Portugal in developing the provinces, and can assist them in training Africans in a large number of different capacities, thus supplementing the limited resources of the motherland.

If we are not to repeat the tragedies of the Congo, Indo-China, and Laos, this war of national liberation must be stopped. The West, and Africans as well, are better served if the chaos of tribal rivalry and Communist-inspired wars of national liberation do not summarily replace *Pax et Imperium!*

CONCLUSION

THE future of multi-racial Africa is in the melting-pot. Great economic advances and the impact of industrialization are everywhere leading to new social tensions. These are made worse because the regions in question are devoid of any national or racial homogeneity. Class conflicts are overlaid and reinforced by racial differences. It is this fact, not any special psychological kinks in settler souls, which makes Rhodesians, Kenyans, and South Africans more prejudiced about each other than, say, Swedes or Englishmen.

At the same time a struggle for power is going on. Africans wish to gain control of the state; they are being resisted by European groups who fear the perils of rapid deterioration of standards, of possible collapse, and the dangers of minority status. In the pursuit of this struggle, the African leaders are playing on the West's guilt-complex about colonialism; they claim to be badly abused, exploited, and neglected, despite the remarkable social and economic progress that has already been achieved within the existing political framework. At the same time, the African leaders face the problem that moderation does not necessarily pay. Some will argue that all would be well, if only their limited political claims were met; but they forget that national movements are apt to increase their demands in geometric progression. It has been almost axiomatic of the struggles of the so-called non-historic nationalities of Eastern Europe that each demand becomes obsolete as soon as it has been conceded; the more moderate leaders who do not adjust themselves to this mounting rhythm are always in danger of being ousted by leaders of a more radical stamp.

The position is further complicated by the imperial factor in British territories. To some extent this too has contributed to the sense of uncertainty that is now being felt in countries like Kenya and the Federation. Imperial intervention, whether from the Right or the Left, is based on the assumption that overseas intervention can still be decisive, despite the fact that

142

Conclusion

in many cases this point of view no longer corresponds to the economic and military realities of the situation. But imperial intervention is still important enough to encourage local politicians to appeal to London rather than to settle their quarrels with each other on the spot. These evasions are not very helpful. For a debate in the United Kingdom Parliament about the affairs of Rhodesia or Kenya often obscures the issues. The real problems involved are not always understood. Instead, British parliamentarians are tempted to give battle on the basis of two opposing political philosophies.

Labour thus calls for democracy, equality, and an end to capitalist exploitation. The Conservatives reply by insisting on limited democracy, liberty, and the virtues of individual economic effort. Both parties conscript the local Africans and Europeans into their ranks, though the people whose interests they respectively sponsor may have nothing in common with their protectors. African congress organizers, or white factory-owners anxious to replace expensive white by cheap black labour, thus do not really fit into the same neat little box marked 'Progressive'. Conservative African chiefs, or European engine-drivers who vote for a right-wing party in Rhodesia, are not Tories.

The political concepts valid in a highly-developed Western European country in fact become quite meaningless when applied in Central Africa. The consequence of using the political phraseology of Western Europe in the political context of Central Africa leads to some very odd results. White entrepreneurs anxious to keep down wages suddenly become left-wing; European workers out to raise their pay sprout forth as right-wingers or conservatives. Jewish immigrants of recent vintage are described as arch-Tory reactionaries, while British bishops 'go left', and are howled down by staunch anti-clericals for undermining society and wrecking the Empire!

This kind of political phrase-mongering can only do harm. Central and Eastern Africa must cease to be an ideological battleground for political parties overseas, or for Pan-African interventions from Ghana and Guinea. East and Central

Africans, white and black alike, have quite enough to cope with at home, without these foreign complications. They must moreover ask for a greater sense of perspective on the part of some of their critics. For when the enormous tensions, real and potential, of their society are taken into consideration, the astonishing thing is not that there have been serious clashes. Surprise should rather be occasioned by the fact that strife up to now has been relatively limited. Europe often forgets how peaceful the African scene is when compared with the bitter, savage, and bloody conflicts, with their mass expulsions and mass slaughter, that have shaken other 'plural societies'.

Africa is not a volcano ready to erupt, it is a continent in the throes of the greatest transformation in its history. There are bound to be conflicts. The most important problem is not so much to do away with them all, for this is an impossible task in any society, but to contain conflict within a peaceful frame-work which will permit of continued economic progress. This is not an easy job; yet we need not be pessimists. The assumption that whites and blacks must inevitably clash is based on the logic of historical determinism. But history provides numerous examples of men accommodating themselves to each other. The Catholic Church learned to live with Protestants, originally on the basis of *apartheid*, expressed in the formula of *cuius regio, eius religio*, later on within the framework of multi-religious states. Communism may possibly be on the road towards accepting the permanence of capitalism within certain regions; Irish people are no longer chased out of the Boston Common; Japanese and Chinese are no longer harassed as they once were in California; Jew-baiting, with some regrettable recent exceptions, has become unpopular in Germany. The conditions of Africans in every country are certainly better now than they have ever been before.* Progress must

* An obvious indicator of social welfare is the average expectation of life of the population. According to figures produced by Dr M. Gelfand, in the U.K. the average expectation of life is 70; in Southern Rhodesia, a white settler country, the African's expectation of life is 48; in Mexico the figure is 39, in Ghana 38, and for Northern Rhodesian Africans it is only 37

144

go on, for it is not only the Europeans' own Western and Christian ideology that makes further reforms inevitable, but also the political realities of African nationalism and the economic realities of an expanding society.

The scope and extent of reform will vary according to the specific situation encountered in the various territories. Certain guiding principles may be acceptable to all. The way to defeat prejudice is to make the contending groups more alike, to promote economic development, and to provide firm and, if necessary, inflexible leadership. The emergence of the new men of Africa must be accepted rather than deplored. The fact that whites and blacks are now contending for the same things proves that they are now involved in the same society, and are quarrelling over the same values of the same culture. This clash represents the painful efforts of both groups to accommodate to each other on a new basis. Even in the Union of South Africa, the principle of *apartheid*, which is inspired by an effort to reduce the areas of clash by territorial separation, can only work ultimately if the black and white areas find some way of collaborating on a territorial, even if not on an individual basis.

North of the Limpopo, policies of partnership on an individual basis have been accepted – at any rate in theory. The 1961 referendum in Southern Rhodesia marked the final parting from South Africa, and a decisive defeat for those who looked southwards for a solution of their problems. Rhodesian politics do not exclude for the time being a considerable degree of segregation for the bulk of the Africans. It tends to be forgotten all too often that segregational methods protect not only the Europeans, but also many Africans. The introduction of an entirely free market in land, for instance, might well lead to the buying up of tribal areas or even of native purchase areas for the benefit of European speculators. The end of all pass legislation again would not necessarily benefit the illiterate Africans unless an acceptable substitute were found, for in an urban environment some means of identification is as necessary for a black as it is for a white worker.

Provision must also be made for the minority of Westernized Africans; and critics of many differing views are agreed that much more needs to be done. Afrikaner nationalists, whilst denying equality to the Bantu middle class in the European areas, are willing to create special 'fiefs' in which advanced Africans will hold local monopolies, a policy which is not without its appeal for some. The Portuguese, on the other hand, are prepared to accept the *assimilado*. British settlers might conceivably fall between two stools. There is much opposition amongst them both to *apartheid* and to assimilation; many have also been too slow to recognize the differentiation that is now taking place within African society and to accept Westernized Africans. Educated black men, however, resent being cooped up with primitive people in African townships. Some praiseworthy attempts have been made to cope with the problem of an African middle class by the provision of separate quarters, but far more remains to be done. The outcry from Westernized Africans might well become smaller if a 'culture bar' were to replace the 'colour bar'.

A compromise based on 'equal rights for equal men' will admittedly be hard to realize. Many Africans distrust the Europeans' intentions; they fear that, as long as the whites are dominant politically, Africans will not be allowed to advance significantly. They complain, not always with a full knowledge of existing constitutional safeguards, that whenever Africans seem about to attain European standards, qualifications are raised to ensure that the whites retain control. They see that some advances have been made in the various multi-racial countries, but regard them as inadequate.

On the European side, fears are equally strong. There is disturbing evidence that an African brand of racism has developed – only the ethnic majority can form a government, only the indigenous people can rule. As one who has felt the oppression of racism in the United States, the Negro journalist Lomax protests that African racism represents change, not progress. It is better for the blacks but worse for the whites, so why should they cooperate? The whites mostly believe that they

Conclusion

cannot concede voting equality without abdicating their future. And African nationalists make the fundamental mistake of attacking the area of greatest white resistance in demanding political power. They would encounter less resistance if they concentrated on social and economic issues first. The black nationalists' habit of talking loudly while carrying a small stick neither conciliates the whites nor frightens them into surrender, but merely encourages them in a policy of resistance. The whites rightly fear the dangers of interim régimes, as well as the preceding period of violence and breakdown of government such as happened in the Congo – despite the optimistic predictions of liberal-minded reformers that all would go well. India from 1945 to 1947 was another example of what could happen. The British no longer dared to stop anyone or anything, with the result that the country of non-violence was shaken by bitter mob-fury. The Weimar Republic in the depression and pre-1948 Palestine suffered similar violence. It is all very well to praise the wisdom of British statesmanship in India, but a price was paid for that wisdom. It was paid by 8,000,000 Indians expelled and hundreds of thousands of dead – it was not paid by London leader-writers.

All the same, there is hope. For however much whites and blacks quarrel, they do at any rate begin to struggle for the same things, the fruits of modern industrial civilization. An expanding economy is forcing both whites and blacks to co-operate on functional lines; the strife for improved living standards in which they both participate forms the cement that holds the plural society together. It is the task of political leaders of whatever persuasion to strengthen these bonds; for the alternative is not some progressive Utopia but a vicious struggle for power. If such a battle should break out, the blacks might win in some regions and the whites in others; there is nothing inevitable about a universal African victory. But whatever the outcome, the ultimate result would be disaster; and welfare, liberty, and the rights of man would alike disappear from the face of the African continent.

FURTHER READING

The standard reference work on Africa is *An African Survey Revised 1956*, by Lord Hailey (Oxford University Press, 1957), a work of encyclopedic proportions. For the pre-conquest history of Africa south of the Sahara, the best available work is D. Westermann's *Geschichte Afrikas: Staatenbildungen südlich der Sahara* (Greven Verlag, Cologne, 1952). The best work available in English is still Sir H. H. Johnston's *History of the Colonization of Africa by Alien Races* (Cambridge University Press, 1899), though much of this is now out of date. *The Partition of Africa*, by J. Keltie Scott (Stanford, 1893), and *The Partition and Colonization of Africa*, by Sir C. Lucas (Oxford University Press, 1922), are also worth consulting. A useful reference work is *An Atlas of African History*, compiled by J. D. Fage (Arnold, 1958), though this requires further expansion. A new general history of Africa is now being prepared by R. Oliver and J. D. Fage.

A major work on the economic history of Africa is S. H. Frankel's *Capital Investment in Africa* (Oxford University Press, 1938), which after more than twenty years is still by far the best in its field. Another brilliant work, which develops the idea of different kinds of economic frontiers, is W. K. Hancock's *Survey of British Commonwealth Affairs*, vol. II, *Problems of Economic Policy 1918-1939* (Oxford University Press, 1942). Other books of economic interest are *Africa: A Social, Economic, and Political Geography of its Major Regions*, by W. Fitzgerald (Methuen, 8th edn, 1957), and a report on *Social Implications of Industrialization and Urbanization in Africa South of the Sahara* (UNESCO, Paris, 1956). Two works selected from the extensive modern literature on the problems of under-developed countries in general are *The Theory of Economic Growth*, by W. A. Lewis (Allen and Unwin, 1955), and *Problems of Capital Formation in Under-Developed Countries*, by R. Nurkse (Blackwell, 3rd edn, 1955).

The general imperial background of colonization is well outlined in *The Cambridge History of the British Empire*, vol. III, edited by E. A. Benians, Sir J. Butler, and C. E. Carrington (Cambridge University Press, 1959), though this concentrates more on the outside

Further Reading

forces impinging on Africa than on developments in the continent itself. A short but brilliant summary of British policy is given by Sir A. Cohen in *British Colonial Policy in Changing Africa* (Routledge and Kegan Paul, 1959); whilst W. M. Macmillan, in *The Road to Self Rule* (Faber and Faber, 1959), a most interesting comparative work, puts forward the view that current academic opinion has now swung far too heavily against the settler. R. L. Buell's *The Native Problem in Africa*, 2 vols. (Macmillan, 1928), is now somewhat out of date but remains a massive compilation. The most up-to-date work on the subject is W. M. Hailey's *Native Administration in the British African Territories*, 5 vols. (H.M.S.O., London, 1950-53), though events have moved so fast that this work too will soon be superseded.

There is no good modern work on the formalized 'treaty' aspect, and the best study is still Sir E. Hertslet's *The Map of Africa by Treaty*, 3 vols. (H.M.S.O., London, 3rd edn, 1909).

Source material for the new 'scramble' for Africa is to be found in C. Bowles's *Africa's Challenge to America* (University of California Press, 1956), which puts forward the liberal point of view. A more general compilation which, for a change, also has a chapter on the vital strategic aspect is *Africa Today*, edited by C. Grove Haines (Johns Hopkins Press, Baltimore, 1955), whilst a briefer discussion is to be found in *The United States and Africa*, edited by W. Goldschmidt (American Assembly, 1958). The standard Russian Communist work on the subject is *Narodi Afriki*, by D. A. Olderogge and I. I. Potekhin (Akademii Nauk, S.S.R., Moscow, 1954), though some of their political conclusions have now been superseded by events. Two recent studies are M. Millikan, *The Emerging Nations: Their Growth and United States Policy* (Little, Brown, 1961), and A. Rivkin, *Western Policy and the New Africa* (T. Hudson, 1961).

SOUTH AFRICAN HISTORY

The literature on the South African historical background is very extensive, the Union being academically the most 'developed' country on the continent. The best English standard work is E. A. Walker's *A History of Southern Africa* (Longmans, revised edn, 1957), which also has a good deal of material on the Federation. An older work is *The Cambridge History of the British Empire*, vol. VIII, edited by A. P. Newton, E. A. Benians, and E. A. Walker (Cambridge University Press, 1936). The standard work in Afrikaans is *Geskiedenis van Suid-Afrika*, 2 vols., edited by A. J. H. van der Walt, J. A. Wiid, and A. L. Geyer (Nasionale Boekhandel, Capetown, 1951).

Special studies on race relations are contained in *Bantu, Boer and Briton* (Faber and Gwyer, 1929) and *The Cape Colour Question* (Faber and Gwyer, 1927), both by W. M. Macmillan; he deals with the making of the problem in early nineteenth-century South Africa from the missionary and humanitarian point of view. Political studies on the question of British northward expansion and the impact of imperial policy are to be found in J. A. I. Agar-Hamilton's *The Road to the North, 1852–86* (Longmans, 1937) and C. W. de Kiewiet's *The Imperial Factor in South Africa* (Cambridge University Press, 1937).

The best general work on South African economic history is C. W. de Kiewiet's *A History of South Africa, Social and Economic* (Oxford University Press, 1950). A most interesting interpretation of the *trek-boer* as a man motivated by economic pressure rather than tradition is to be found in S. D. Neumark's *Economic Influences on the South African Frontier, 1652–1836* (Stanford University Press, 1957). The most brilliant work in this field is P. J. van der Merwe's *Trek: Studies oor die Mobiliteit van die Pioniersbevolking aan die Kaap* (Nasionale Pers Beperk, Capetown, 1945).

MISSION HISTORY

Literature on this subject is extensive, but the best general standard works are J. du Plessis's *A History of Christian Missions in South Africa* (Longmans, 1911) and C. P. Groves's *The Planting of Christianity in Africa*, vol. III, 1878–1914 (Lutterworth Press, 1955). Catholic missions have been given special consideration by A. da Silva Rego in *Curso de Missionologia* (Agência Geral do Ultramar, Lisbon, 1956). The best work on East African and Nyasaland mission history, R. Oliver's *The Missionary Factor in East Africa* (Longmans, 1952), also contains valuable interpretative material. R. Slade has produced an interesting specialist study of *English-Speaking Missions in the Congo Independent State, 1878 to 1908* (Académie Royale des Sciences Coloniales, Brussels, 1959).

The best available works on the subject of African separatist churches in South Africa are B. G. M. Sundkler's *Bantu Prophets in South Africa* (Lutterworth Press, 1948) and K. Schlosser's *Eingeborenenkirchen in Süd- und Südwestafrika* (W. G. Mühlau, Kiel,

Further Reading

1958). An extremely detailed and scholarly account of the impact of Christian mission work on incipient African nationalism is to be found in *Independent African: John Chilembwe and the Origins, Setting, and Significance of the Nyasaland Native Rising of 1915*, by G. Shepperson and T. Price (Edinburgh University Press, 1958).

AFRICAN NATIONALISM

The best general account is T. Hodgkin's *Nationalism in Colonial Africa* (Muller, 1956). A Rhodesian African's view has been put forward by N. Sithole in *African Nationalism* (Oxford University Press, 1958). These works should be studied in connexion with *The Idea of Colonialism*, edited by R. Strausz Hupé and H. Hazard (Praeger, 1958), especially noting the brilliant and penetrating contribution by H. Kohn, a specialist on European nationalism who is very critical of the 'anti-colonialist' school. L. H. Gann has criticized some of the ideas animating European liberal supporters of African nationalism in South Africa in an article, 'Liberal Interpretations of South African History', in *Rhodes-Livingstone Journal*, No. 25, 1960; by contrast, a European supporter of the former Nyasaland African National Congress, Guy Clutton-Brock, has put forward the point of view of a Christian Socialist in *Dawn in Nyasaland* (Hodder and Stoughton, 1959). Detailed studies of the Kikuyu problem in Kenya are to be found in L. S. B. Leakey's *Mau Mau and the Kikuyu* (Methuen, 1952), while another European, J. C. Carothers, has made a study of *The Psychology of Mau Mau* (Government Printer, Nairobi, 1955). J. Kenyatta's *Facing Mount Kenya* (Secker and Warburg, 1953) presents a very idealized picture of the African past. A valuable, detailed study of African nationalism and trade unionism in Luanshya, a town on the Northern Rhodesian Copper Belt, is to be found in A. L. Epstein's *Politics in an Urban African Community* (Manchester University Press, 1958). Also of considerable merit is J. A. Barnes's study of the history and present condition of a former warrior-people, *Politics in a Changing Society: A Political History of the Fort Jameson Ngoni* (Oxford University Press, 1954).

RACE RELATIONS

The literature is an extensive one. Unfortunately the study of race relations has all too often been arbitrarily confined to the relations of European and African races, instead of taking in the whole sub-

151

White Settlers in Tropical Africa

ject of clashes between ethnic groups in general, with the result that all too many scholars have tended to see the problem as one in 'black and white'.

Two books worth consulting are G. W. Allport's *The Nature of Prejudice* (Doubleday, New York, 1958) and Sir A. Burns's *Colour Prejudice: With Particular Reference to Relationships between Whites and Negroes* (Allen and Unwin, 1948). W. J. Cash's *The Mind of the South* (Doubleday, New York, 1954) is a brilliant study of the American 'Deep South'; G. Freyre, in *The Masters and the Slaves: A Study of Brazilian Civilization* (Knopf, New York, 1946), stresses sexual factors, whilst F. Tannenbaum, in *Slave and Citizen: The Negro in the Americas* (Knopf, 1947), places more emphasis on religious and legal factors in the formation of race attitudes. A most valuable work of reference for South Africa is the *Handbook on Race Relations in South Africa*, edited by E. Hellmann (Oxford University Press, 1949). H. Kuper's *The Uniform of Colour: A Study of White-Black Relationships in Swaziland* (Witwatersrand University Press, 1947) is an interesting specialist study, and so is M. Gluckman's 'Analysis of a Social Situation in Modern Zululand', in *Bantu Studies*, vol. 13, 1939, pp. 1-30, 147-74. A modern work by the same author is *Custom and Conflict in Africa* (Blackwell, 1955), whilst he has also made a brilliant interpretative study of judicial and psychological factors in African life – which are often misunderstood – in *The Judicial Process among the Barotse of Northern Rhodesia*, by M. Gluckman (Manchester University Press, 1955). *Race Attitudes in South Africa: Historical, Experimental, and Psychological Studies* (Witwatersrand University Press, 1957) by I. D. MacCrone, a psychologist, has an excellent historical section, but some of the findings on 'inter-white' social attitudes are out of date now, since the book was first published in 1937. D. C. Mannoni's *Prospero and Caliban: The Psychology of Colonization*, translated by P. Powesland (Methuen, 1956), gives an individual interpretation of the settler mind. R. Maunier's *The Sociology of Colonies: An Introduction to the Study of Race Contacts*, edited and translated by E. O. Lorimer, 2 vols. (Routledge and Kegan Paul, 1949), stands in a very different category. A more popular work is A. H. Richmond's *The Colour Problem: A Study of Racial Relations* (Penguin Books, 1955). Also worth consulting are G. Saenger's *The Social Psychology of Prejudice* (Harper, New York, 1953) and J. H. Oldham's *New Hope in Africa: The Aims of the Capricorn Africa Society* (Longmans, 1955). The views of South African Nationalists are put for-

Further Reading

ward in the publications of the South African Bureau of Racial Affairs, Stellenbosch, whilst the liberal point of view is presented by the South African Institute of Race Relations at Johannesburg, and by the Institute of Race Relations, London. The views of an Afrikaans-speaking liberal churchman are given by B. J. Marais in *Colour: Unsolved Problem of the West* (Timmins, Cape Town, 1952).

SPECIFIC TERRITORIES

Ex-Belgian Congo

The material in English on the Congo is not very comprehensive. The best general work of reference is *Encyclopédie du Congo Belge* (Éditions Bieleveld, *c.* 1958), but it would also be worth consulting R. Meyer's *Introduction au Congo Belge et au Ruanda-Urundi* (Office de Publicité, Brussels, 1955). P. Ryckmans, in *La Politique Coloniale* (Édition Rex, Louvain, 1934) and *Dominer pour servir* (Édition Universelle, revised edn, 1948), discusses the more general significance of colonies and the Belgian version of the trusteeship principle. Other works are R. Schreyven's *Et le Congo* (Brussels, 1957) which contains a collection of articles from *La Libre Belgique*, E. Verleyen's *Congo: Patrimoine de la Belgique* (De Visscher, Brussels, 1950). The recent trouble in the Congo is discussed in Colin Legum's *Congo Disaster* (Penguin Books, 1961), R. Calder's *Agony of the Congo* (Gollancz, 1961), and A. Merriam's *Congo: Background of Conflict* (North-western University Press, 1961).

Kenya and the East African Background

Indispensable for the historical background of the region as a whole is R. Coupland's *The Exploitation of East Africa: 1856-90, the Slave Trade and the Scramble* (Faber and Faber, 1939) and, by the same author, *East Africa and Its Invaders* (Oxford University Press, 1956). F. D. Lugard's *The Rise of Our East African Empire*, 2 vols. (Blackwood, 1893), is written from the point of view of one of the participants; his standard biography, by M. Perham, runs to two volumes; *Lugard, The Years of Adventure, 1858-1898* (Collins, 1956), and *Lugard, The Years of Authority, 1898-1945* (Collins, 1960).

A brief general work on the area is *An Introduction to the History of East Africa*, by Z. Marsh and G. W. Kingsnorth (Cambridge University Press, 1957), whilst a more scholarly work is R. Reusch's *History of East Africa* (F. Unger, revised edn, 1961).

White Settlers in Tropical Africa

E. Huxley and M. Perham present *Race and Politics in Kenya* (Faber and Faber, revised edn, 1956) as a discussion in the form of letters, one of the authors taking the part of the white settlers, whilst the other opposes them. Also worth studying is *Settlers of Kenya* (Longmans, 1948), by E. Huxley, whose *White Man's Country: Lord Delamere and the Making of Kenya* (Macmillan, 1935) is still the finest existing work on the subject. A critical study of government, missionaries, and settlers is given by L. S. B. Leakey in *Kenya Contrasts and Problems* (Methuen, 1936), whilst N. Leys's *Kenya* (Hogarth Press, 1924) represents an early left-wing attack on the settlers. More recent works are J. F. Lipscomb's *White Africans* (Faber and Faber, 1954), M. Macmillan's *Introducing East Africa* (Faber and Faber, 1952), and D. H. Rawcliffe's *The Struggle for Kenya* (Gollancz, 1954). A good general account of East Africa is R. Wraith's *East African Citizen* (Oxford University Press, 1959), while recent political and social events are treated by S. Wood in *Kenya: The Tensions of Progress* (Oxford University Press, 1960). Works bearing on the Mau Mau rising have already been mentioned under the section dealing with African nationalism.

Tanganyika and Uganda

There is no standard history of Tanganyika as such, apart from general works on East Africa, but an interesting book is *My Tanganyika Service and Some Nigeria* (Allen and Unwin, 1939), by Sir D. C. Cameron, the Governor who laid the foundations of British mandatory policy there. P. Clarke's *A Short History of Tanganyika* (Longmans, Green, 1960) is readable. A standard reference work is J. O. Moffatt's *Handbook of Tanganyika* (Government Printer, Dar-es-Salaam, 2nd edn, 1958). A Rhodesian African trained in political science, B. T. G. Chidzero, has analysed political and constitutional development in *Tanganyika and International Trusteeship* (Oxford University Press, 1961).

K. Ingham's *The Making of Modern Uganda* (Allen and Unwin, 1958) is the recognized standard work on the subject, though *Uganda*, by H. B. Thomas and R. Scott (Oxford University Press, 1935), is also still worth consulting. W. H. Ingrams's *Uganda: A Crisis of Nationhood* (H.M.S.O., 1960) surveys current problems. A. W. Southall and P. C. W. Gutkind have produced an interesting specialist study of 'Townsmen in the Making: Kampala and Its Suburbs' (*East African Studies*, No. 9, 1956), which gives details concerning

Further Reading

labour-migration and the lack of urban stability in an African country where there are no settlers, no segregation, and no Land Apportionment Act; this should be read by all who make the conventional criticisms of South Africa and Rhodesia.

Portuguese Africa

The literature available in English is limited, but two interesting doctoral dissertations may be consulted: E. V. Axelson's *South-East Africa, 1488-1530* (Longman's 1940), and M. V. Jackson's *European Powers and South-East Africa* (Longmans, 1942). More modern works are J. Duffy's *Portuguese Africa* (Harvard University Press, 1959), F. C. C. Egerton's *Angola in Perspective* (Routledge and Kegan Paul, 1957), M. Harris's *Portugal's African 'Wards'* (American Committee on Africa, New York, 1958), and C. F. Spence's *The Portuguese Colony of Moçambique* (Balkema, 1951). A massive series on Portuguese colonial history has been written by S. R. Welch, an English Catholic Father; particularly interesting is his *Portuguese and Dutch in South Africa, 1641-1806* (Juta, 1951).

The literature in Portuguese is very considerable and one might perhaps select from it four useful works: A. M. Afonso's *Princípios Fundamentais de Organização Política e Administrativa* (Lisbon, 1956), *Do Conselho Ultramarino ao Conselho do Império* (Lisbon, 1943), by M. Caetano, who has also written *Tradição, Princípios, e Métodos da Colonização Portuguesa* (Agência Geral do Ultramar, 1951), and A. A. Felner's *Angola: Apontamentos sôbre a Colonização dos Planaltos e Litoral do Sul de Angola* (Agência Geral, 1940), a study of white settlement in the highlands of Southern Angola. M. S. Vaz, in *Problemas de Moçambique* (Lourenço Marques, 1951), is more critical than most Portuguese authors. Also worth reading, from the historical point of view, is E. de Vilhena's *O Regime dos Prazos da Zambezia* (Lisbon, 1916). A modern historical work of considerable merit is A. Lobato's *A Expansão Portuguesa em Moçambique de 1498 a 1530* (Agência Geral, 1954) an older and more comprehensive work being J. J. T. Botelho's *História Militar e Política dos Portugueses em Moçambique*, 2 vols. (Centro Tipográfico Colonial, 1934-6).

Federation of Rhodesia and Nyasaland

The standard work of reference is the *Handbook for the Federation of Rhodesia and Nyasaland*, edited by V. Brelsford (Government

Printer, Salisbury, 1960). The anthropological background to the area has been unusually well covered in the publications of the Rhodes-Livingstone Institute, Lusaka, which is now also conducting a psychological and sociological study of European colonists by J. McEwan. Political and administrative aspects have been dealt with by J. W. Davidson in *The Northern Rhodesian Legislative Council* (Faber and Faber, 1948), and by C. Leys in *European Politics in Southern Rhodesia* (Clarendon Press, 1959), an interesting study by a political scientist with Fabian sympathies. H. Rolin's *Les Lois et l'administration de la Rhodésie* (Bruylant, Brussels, 1913) is a brilliant and thorough account of early administrative problems in Rhodesia. Various aspects of African nationalism are dealt with in the books by A. L. Epstein, G. Shepperson and T. Price, and J. A. Barnes which have already been mentioned. In a specialist study of Northern Rhodesia, *The Birth of a Plural Society* (Manchester University Press, 1958), L. H. Gann attempts to blend the sociological and the historical approach to race relations. P. Mason gives a more general account in *The Birth of a Dilemma: The Conquest and Settlement of Rhodesia* (Oxford University Press, 1958), and the story is brought up to date by R. Grey in *The Two Nations* (Oxford University Press, 1960). A general historical introduction from the imperial point of view is A. J. Hanna's *The Beginnings of Nyasaland and North-Eastern Rhodesia, 1859-1895* (Clarendon Press, 1956), whilst *The Making of Rhodesia* (Macmillan, 1926), by H. M. Hole, an ex-Chartered Company civil servant, is still the standard history of Southern Rhodesia. An excellent detailed study is *Sir Harry Johnston and the Scramble for Africa,* by R. Oliver (Chatto and Windus, 1957); two popular works are *Zambezi Sunrise: How Civilization Came to Rhodesia and Nyasaland,* by W. D. Gale (Timmins, 1958), and *The Rhodesian: The Life of Sir Roy Welensky* by D. Taylor (Museum Press, 1955). The biography of Southern Rhodesia's first Prime Minister is recorded by J. P. R. Wallis in *One Man's Hand: The Story of Sir Charles Coghlan and the Liberation of Southern Rhodesia* (Longmans, 1950).

The literature on Rhodes is tremendous, the most readable and, at the same time, scholarly work being B. Williams's *Cecil Rhodes* (Constable, 1938 edn). An important though little publicized aspect of colonial history is covered by Dr M. Gelfand in *Tropical Victory: An Account of the Influence of Medicine on the History of Southern Rhodesia, 1890-1923* (Juta, 1953). Outstanding amongst the vast body of literature on Livingstone is the same author's *Livingstone*

Further Reading

the Doctor: His Life and Travels, A Study in Medical History (Black-well, 1957). The penetration of early Rhodesia by white hunters and traders from the south is outlined by E. C. Tabler in *The Far Interior* (Balkema, 1955), whilst C. H. Thompson and H. W. Woodruff deal with more general economic problems in *Economic Development in Rhodesia and Nyasaland* (Dobson, 1954).

On developments since Federation, the following six books are useful: E. M. Clegg, *Race and Politics: Partnership in the Federation of Rhodesia and Nyasaland* (Oxford University Press, 1960); T. R. M. Creighton, *The Anatomy of Partnership: Southern Rhodesia and the Central African Federation* (Faber and Faber, 1960); A. Hazlewood and P. D. Henderson, *Nyasaland: The Economics of Federation* (Blackwell, 1960); C. Leys and C. Pratt, *A New Deal in Central Africa* (Heinemann, 1960); P. Mason, *Year of Decision: Rhodesia and Nyasaland in 1960* (Oxford University Press, 1960); and C. Sanger, *Central African Emergency* (Heinemann, 1960).

APPENDIX

SOME FACTS AND FIGURES
CONCERNING WHITE SETTLEMENT

THIS background material does not in any way purport to be exhaustive, partly for reasons of space, and partly because the statistical information available on the whites in the different territories varies greatly in arrangement, availability, and quality.

The information provided is in the main drawn from the Central African Statistical Office, the East African Statistical Department, and the Repartição de Estatisticas Geral, Angola. Use has also been made of the *Statesman's Year Book*. In view of the importance of the Federation's white population, more attention has been devoted to this than to any other area of white settlement.

'European' is here synonymous with 'white', and includes, for example, Americans and all white South Africans.

FEDERATION OF RHODESIA AND NYASALAND

1. The area of the Federation as a whole amounts to 478,030 sq. miles: Southern Rhodesia, 150,333 sq. miles; Northern Rhodesia, 290,323 sq.miles; Nyasaland, 37,374 sq. miles.

2. The African population of the Federation in 1958 amounted to 7,560,000: Southern Rhodesia, 2,590,000; Northern Rhodesia, 2,250,000; Nyasaland, 2,720,000.

3. European population growth in the three Central African territories:

Year	Northern Rhodesia	Southern Rhodesia	Nyasaland	Total
1901	—	11,032	314	11,346
1911	1,497	23,606	766	25,869
1921	3,634	33,620	1,486	38,740
1931	13,846	49,910	1,975	65,731
1946	21,907	82,386	2,400	106,693
1951	37,221	136,017	4,073	177,311

Appendix

Year	Northern Rhodesia	Southern Rhodesia	Nyasaland	Total
After Federation				
1955	58,000	165,000	5,800	228,800
1956	66,000	178,000	6,800	250,800
1957	72,000	193,000	7,500	272,500
1958	72,000	207,000	8,300	287,300
1959	73,000	215,000	8,800	296,800
1960	76,000	223,000	9,300	308,800

4. Since 1951 the European population has grown at an average compound rate of 6.5 per cent per annum. During the same period the African population has grown at a corresponding rate of 2.5 per cent.

5. European population growth in the main towns of the Federation:

Town	May 1956 Census	December 1957 Estimate	December 1960 Estimate
SOUTHERN RHODESIA			
Salisbury	61,930	76,000	86,000
Bulawayo	41,287	47,000	52,000
Umtali	7,051	7,700	8,400
Gwelo	5,832	6,400	7,000
Que Que	1,918	2,100	2,300
Gatooma	1,622	1,900	2,100
Fort Victoria	1,396	1,600	1,900
NORTHERN RHODESIA			
Lusaka	9,449	11,000	11,900
Kitwe-Nkana	9,805	10,600	10,800
Ndola	7,384	8,000	9,300
Mufulira	5,730	6,100	6,600
Luanshya–Roan Antelope	6,161	6,400	6,400
Chingola–Nchanga	4,851	5,200	5,200
Broken Hill	4,250	4,500	4,500
Livingstone	3,673	3,900	4,000
Bancroft	1,787	—	2,200
NYASALAND			
Blantyre–Limbe	2,457	3,000	3,800

6. The above seventeen towns contained approximately 72 per cent of the total European population of the Federation in 1960.

Appendix

7. Migration of Europeans, exclusive of movements within the Federation:

Territory	1957	1958	1959
SOUTHERN RHODESIA			
Immigration	17,400	12,900	8,100
Estimated emigration	5,100	5,300	4,400
Estimated net immigration	12,300	7,600	3,700
NORTHERN RHODESIA			
Immigration	6,800	4,000	4,100
Estimated emigration	5,200	7,300	3,200
Estimated net immigration	1,600	—3,300	900
NYASALAND			
Immigration	800	700	600
Estimated emigration	400	200	400
Estimated net immigration	400	500	200
FEDERATION TOTAL			
Immigration	25,000	17,600	12,800
Estimated emigration	10,700	12,800	8,000
Estimated net immigration	14,300	4,800	4,800

8. Principal nationalities of 'European' immigrants in 1958:

BRITISH		14,317
Born in the U.K. and Irish Republic	8,453	
Born in the Union of South Africa	5,040	
Others British by birth	736	
Naturalized	88	
FOREIGNERS		2,162
Hollanders	653	
Italians	489	
Portuguese	197	
Americans	167	
Germans	166	
Greeks	75	
Austrians	62	
Swiss	50	
Israelis	45	
Hungarians	44	
Yugoslavs	40	
Poles	33	
Danes	30	
Others	111	
TOTAL EUROPEANS		16,479

Appendix

9. In 1958 51 per cent of the European immigrants were citizens of the United Kingdom, 31 per cent were citizens of the Union of South Africa, and 13 per cent were citizens of foreign, i.e, non-Commonwealth countries.

10. Industrial distribution of Europeans in employment in the Federation:

	1956	1960
Commerce and finance	25,366	29,260
Manufacturing and refining	14,423	19,240
Construction work	13,381	12,370
Transport and communications	10,723	12,000
Mining and quarrying	9,790	10,740
Agriculture, forestry, and fishing	9,321	5,280
Government administrative services	9,672	} 33,980
Medical and educational services	7,423	
Other services	8,999	
Electricity, water, and sanitation	1,443	1,940
Not classified	1,212	—

11. Changes in the industrial distribution of Europeans in employment in Southern Rhodesia (the main centre of white settlement in the Federation). Census figures include employers and employed; later estimates cover employed only.

	1951 Census	1956 Census	1959 Estimate	1960 Estimate
Commerce	11,322	19,672	23,270	24,070
Services	15,058	17,975	22,020	23,300
Manufacturing	9,920	11,561	15,110	15,710
Transport and communications	5,325	7,810	9,300	8,840
Construction	7,622	9,095	9,140	8,340
Agriculture	7,129	7,669	4,060	4,070
Mining and quarrying	2,708	3,097	2,870	2,750
Electricity and water	773	1,195	1,460	1,540
Total:	59,857	78,074	87,230	88,620

12. Enrolment of European school children in 1958:

	Southern Rhodesia	Northern Rhodesia
Primary schools	28,951	10,475
Secondary schools	11,947	3,301

Appendix

13. National income of the Federation:

	1954	1955	1956	1957	1958	1959
			(£ thousand)			
Wages and salaries:						
European	85,501	99,856	113,705	126,723	135,551	140,532
Asian and Coloured	2,276	2,501	2,773	3,177	3,690	3,915
African	53,712	61,352	69,968	80,231	81,313	87,243
Total:	141,489	163,709	186,446	210,131	220,554	231,690
Income from unin-corporated enterprise:						
European	22,270	23,852	24,550	25,109	25,024	25,343
Asian and Coloured	3,245	3,579	4,071	4,295	4,495	4,767
African: Subsistence	69,343	70,032	72,137	75,290	80,628	85,085
Other	9,009	9,224	12,490	13,059	11,015	13,815
Total:	103,867	106,687	113,248	117,753	121,162	129,010
Net operating profits:						
Companies	78,154	96,576	107,524	71,212	55,935	96,019
Statutory bodies	4,138	5,032	6,256	6,929	5,453	5,972
Government income from property:						
Profits	2,620	3,205	3,903	4,827	5,853	6,522
Rent	1,669	1,628	1,737	1,972	2,181	2,500
Royalties	2,248	2,626	3,796	2,846	2,076	2,984
Personal income from property	4,447	5,106	5,369	5,463	6,051	6,308
Net domestic product at factor cost	338,632	384,569	428,279	421,133	419,265	481,005
Less: Net income paid abroad	—35,100	—39,447	—46,852	—40,776	—30,593	—41,183
Net national product at factor cost	303,532	345,122	381,427	380,357	388,672	439,822
Plus: Sums set aside for depreciation	20,968	25,157	28,486	29,267	29,983	32,761
Gross national product at factor cost	324,500	370,279	409,913	409,624	418,655	472,583
Plus: Indirect taxes	13,685	17,109	22,304	25,399	26,955	27,749
Less: Subsidies	—2,979	—3,241	—2,319	—4,147	—4,449	—2,238
Gross national product at market prices	335,206	384,147	429,898	430,876	441,161	498,094

14. Saving and investment in the Federation (£ *thousand*):

	1954	1955	1956	1957	1958	1959
Provision for depreciation:						
Statutory bodies	1,878	2,443	2,852	3,102	3,671	4,028
Companies	12,067	15,191	17,404	17,468	17,170	18,987
Personal	7,023	7,523	8,230	8,697	9,142	9,746
Total:	20,968	25,157	28,486	29,267	29,983	32,761
Saving:						
Central government	14,159	22,494	26,859	28,976	18,283	12,138
Local government	2,442	3,077	4,132	4,739	4,823	4,820
Statutory bodies	3,453	3,703	3,238	3,427	463	—1,033
Companies	21,665	27,378	26,546	—6,645	—560	34,849
Personal	13,542	20,690	31,042	29,086	24,932	31,408
Total:	55,261	77,342	91,817	59,583	47,941	82,182
Total domestic saving	76,229	102,499	120,303	88,850	77,924	114,943
Borrowing abroad:						
1. Net capital inflow:						
Government	14,935	8,895	1,516	—1,234	13,544	9,249
Statutory bodies	—8	488	2,828	6,903	11,434	9,701
Private	6,219	25,550	28,763	22,056	39,049	21,974
Total:	21,146	34,933	33,107	27,725	64,027	40,924
2. Net drawing on external balances:						
Government	2,009	—6,565	2,232	5,085	—2,450	—1,097
Statutory bodies	3,122	—855	—3,462	1,546	—308	—626
Companies	—8,982	—18,622	14,484	29,485	3,696	—22,420
Banking reserves	—3,156	7,216	—8,362	10,632	—2,071	2,167
Total:	—7,007	—18,826	4,892	46,748	—1,133	—21,976
Total net borrowing from abroad:	14,139	16,107	37,999	74,473	62,894	18,948
Gross domestic capital formation	90,368	118,606	158,302	163,323	140,818	133,891

15. During the whole period 1954 to 1959, gross domestic capital formation amounted to more than £805 million; of this, nearly £581 million was financed by domestic saving and less than £225 million by net borrowing abroad.

Appendix

KENYA

1. The area of Kenya amounts to 224,960 sq. miles. Its total estimated population in 1960 was 6,550,700, of whom 6,264,000 were Africans and 67,700 were Europeans.

2. In 1911 there were 3,175 Europeans in Kenya, by 1921 there were 9,651, and by 1931 there were 16,812. The following figures give estimates of the European civil population since the Second World War, and the number of new permanent European immigrants:

Year	Total Europeans	Permanent Immigrants
1946	24,900	3,509
1947	27,500	5,040
1948	30,800	6,501
1949	33,800	4,968
1950	36,600	3,503
1951	38,600	3,719
1952	40,700	3,827
1953	42,200	4,781
1954	47,900	4,904
1955	52,500	5,715
1956	57,700	4,553
1957	62,700	3,148
1958	64,700	2,818
1959	66,400	3,058
1960	67,700	2,167

3. The following tables give a breakdown of the 1957 white immigrants to Kenya by age, sex, and occupation:

Age	Male	Female	Total
0–4	219	273	492
5–14	341	300	641
15–19	64	74	138
20–29	872	835	1,707
30–39	737	635	1,372
40–49	371	237	608
50 and over	168	191	359
Not stated	115	109	224
Total	2,887	2,654	5,541

Appendix

Occupation	Male	Female	Total
Agriculture	127	2	129
Metal workers	175	2	177
Wood and furniture	32	—	32
Builders and bricklayers	61	2	63
Government service	446	104	550
Military service	22	1	23
Commercial, financial, and insurance	368	11	379
Professional	328	295	623
Clerks, draughtsmen, typists (not Government)	115	150	265
Other occupations	425	92	517
Retired, not employed (including women and children)	648	1,893	2,541
Not stated	140	102	242
Total	**2,887**	**2,645**	**5,541**

TANGANYIKA

1. The area of Tanganyika amounts to 362,688 sq. miles. Its total estimated population in 1960 was 9,238,600, of whom 9,099,000 were Africans and 22,300 were Europeans.

2. The following figures illustrate the growth of the European population since 1913:

1913	5,336	1956	20,200
1921	2,447	1958	21,200
1931	8,228	1960	22,300
1948	11,300		

The low figure for 1921 was due to the loss of many German-speaking settlers after the First World War.

3. Immigration of Europeans since 1949:

1949	4,313	1956	2,581
1953	2,628	1957	2,679
1954	2,603	1958	1,897
1955	3,112	1959	1,918

Appendix

4. According to the 1957 census, approximately 50 per cent of the white population was classified as urban. The main centres were: Dar-es-Salaam, 4,479; Arusha, 878; Tanga, 768; Moshi, 441. The number of civil servants amounted to 2,522.

5. The following is a breakdown of the white population in 1957 by age and sex:

Age	Male	Female	Total
0–9	2,354	2,222	4,576
10–19	692	653	1,345
20–29	1,557	1,424	2,981
30–39	2,685	2,394	5,079
40–49	2,153	1,509	3,662
50 and over	1,611	1,171	2,782
Not stated	56	53	109
Total	11,108	9,426	20,534

OVERSEAS PROVINCES OF PORTUGAL –
PORTUGUESE GUINEA, ANGOLA, AND MOÇAMBIQUE

European migration to and from the Overseas Provinces of Portugal as a whole since 1937:

Year	Departures Men			Entries Men			Balance of Settlers	
	Total	No.	%	Total	No.	%	Total	Men
1937	4,895	3,041	62·1	4,004	2,463	61·5	891	578
1941	5,547	3,173	57·2	3,266	2,083	63·8	2,281	1,090
1945	9,441	5,767	61·1	6,905	3,873	56·1	2,536	1,894
1949	16,456	10,003	60·8	8,893	5,080	57·1	7,563	4,923
1953	23,665	13,260	56·0	12,350	7,167	57·1	11,315	6,093
1957	27,289	15,107	55·4	16,937	9,594	56·6	10,352	5,513

PORTUGUESE GUINEA

The area of Portuguese Guinea amounts to 13,948 sq. miles. Its total estimated population in 1959 was 565,000, including over 2,000 Europeans.

Appendix

1. The area of Angola amounts to 481,351 sq. miles. The total estimated population in 1959 was 4,550,000, of whom over 160,000 were Europeans.

2. The following figures illustrate the growth of the European population since 1940:

1940	44,083	1954	122,484
1950	78,826	1955	134,690
1951	88,163	1956	146,461
1952	100,332	1957	156,703
1953	110,035		

3. In 1955 the main centres of European population were as follows:

Luanda	34,250
Lobito	6,390
Benguela	3,400

4. The following figures give a breakdown of the white population first by age and sex, then by educational status, according to the census of 1950 in Angola:

Age	Male	Female	Total
0–9	8,181	9,319	17,500
10–19	6,746	5,976	12,722
20–29	10,191	6,741	16,932
30–39	8,616	5,285	13,901
40–49	5,825	3,191	9,016
50 and over	5,028	2,855	7,883

Educational status	Male	Female	Total
Unable to read or write	8,753	9,400	18,153
Able to read and write	12,613	9,571	22,184
Primary education only	16,340	10,702	27,042
Secondary education	6,967	3,091	10,058
Higher education	1,162	227	1,389

1. The area of Moçambique amounts to 297,731 sq. miles. The total estimated population in 1959 was over 6,300,000. In 1950 the total population was 5,738,911.

Appendix

2. The following figures illustrate the growth of the European population since 1928:

1928	17,842	1953	60,249
1940	27,438	1954	64,529
1945	31,221	1955	67,798
1950	48,213	1956	74,600
1951	52,008	1957	80,200
1952	56,647		

3. The main European nationalities in 1955 were as follows:

Portuguese	63,386
British	457
South Africans	368
Italians	359
Greeks	307
Germans	306

4. The main centres of European population in 1955 were Lourenço Marques, 28,301, and Beira, 10,306.

EX-BELGIAN CONGO

1. The area of the Belgian Congo amounted to *c.* 902,000 sq. miles. It is estimated that the total population in 1958 was approximately 13,000,000, of whom 109,457 were Europeans.

2. The main European nationalities represented in the Congo in 1956 were as follows:

Belgians	84,444
Portuguese	5,300
Italians	3,364
Greeks	3,177
British	2,236
French	2,247
Americans	1,793
Dutch	1,357
Swiss	825
Luxemburgers	539
South Africans	263
Swedes	224
Canadians	178
Germans	152
Spaniards	148
Poles	144

Appendix

3. The following figures give an approximate idea of the main European occupations in 1958:

Civil servants	9,382
Businessmen	20,307
Settlers	9,621
Technicians and clerks	62,994
Missionaries	7,131

4. The main centres of European population in 1956 were as follows:

Leopoldville	20,982
Elizabethville	13,808
Stanleyville	5,095
Jadotville	4,782
Bukavu	4,327
Kolwesi	4,042
Luluabourg	3,228

5. Since 1960 the European population has been sharply diminished by mass emigration. The exact number of Europeans left in the Congo in 1961 was unknown, but some 10,000 were estimated to have remained in Katanga Province.

RUANDA-URUNDI

1. The area of Ruanda-Urundi amounts to 19,536 sq. miles. The total estimated population is approximately 4,500,000.

2. In 1955 the total white population was over 6,000, of whom 2,643 were living in Usumbura, the main town.